In Season

Embracing the Father's Process of Fruitfulness

WAYNE JACOBSEN

Trailview Media
Newbury Park, CA

In Season by Wayne Jacobsen

International Standard Book Number
978-0-9839491-1-4

Cover design: nbishopsdesigns.com
Cover photo: Istockphoto © mbbirdy

Trailview Media an imprint of Lifestream
www.lifestream.org
1560-1 Newbury Rd, #313
Newbury Park, CA 91320
(805) 498-7774
fax: (805) 499-5975
office@lifestream.org

Printed in the United States of America

Dedication

To my father and mother
GENE AND JO JACOBSEN
Who first introduced me to God as a real presence in the
universe and showed me how to trust his unfolding work and
to rest from my own.

And to parents like them everywhere, who seek to encourage
their children on a similar journey.

Contents

Introduction 8

  1. An Amazing Invitation 11
  2. In My Father's Vineyard 16
  3. The Seasons of the Vineyard 22

Spring: New Life Begins

  4. Hope Springs Eternal 31
  5. A Father You Can Trust 33
  6. I've Been Chosen 39
  7. You Are Already Clean 45
  8. Training the New Vine 50
  9. Blossoms of Promise 55
 10. A Way to Live 61
 11. A Life-Long Friendship 67
 12. Of Fading Blossoms and Future Fruit 72

Summer: The Fruit Matures

 13. The Long, Hot Days of Summer 79
 14. The Upside of Trouble 83
 15. The Faithful Provider 89
 16. A Peek at God's Priorities 94
 17. What Do You Mean, Fruitful? 98
 18. If You 103
 19. What About the Unfruitful Branch? 107
 20. Life Giving Nourishment 111
 21. Enemies of Maturity 116
 22. The Farmer's Diligence 121
 23. Having Done All, Stand! 125
 24. Softer and Sweeter 129

Fall: Harvest Time

25. The Joys of Harvest 135
26. Out of Water, Wine! 138
27. Whatever I Ask? 143
28. The Fruit Tells All 148
29. Look at the Fields! 153
30. Just Whose Fruit Is It Anyway? 158
31. What Happens When There Is No Harvest? 162
32. The Growing Is Not Yet Over 166

Winter: Resting and Restaging

33. Days of Rest and Preparation 173
34. Fading Glory 175
35. The Colder the Better 179
36. The Pause That Refreshes 183
37. Submitting to the Master's Pruning 186
38. Die to It 191
39. Trained Up for Fruitfulness 197
40. Go and Bear Fruit 202

Introduction

A Personal Time Warp

I do not consider myself yet to have taken hold of it.
But one thing I do: Forgetting what is behind and
straining toward what is ahead, I press on toward the goal to win the
prize for which God has called me heavenward in Christ Jesus.
PHILIPPIANS 3:13-14

I'll admit I have a problem. I can't just rerelease another edition of a book without tinkering with it.

I see life as a journey, and any book, audio, or article is just a snapshot of that journey. So while what I wrote twenty years ago was the best I knew then, God's work has continued to shape my life. I would not write the same book today. So putting out a new edition of a book I wrote in the distant past, even if it was one of my favorites, is not as easy as simply sending it to the printers again.

I knew the book needed to be changed. What I wasn't prepared for was how much it needed changing. As I read it over I knew printing it as it was would be like posting my high school photo on my home page. Sure the resemblance is there, but I don't think anyone would see that photo and know immediately that it was me. I have changed a lot since high school. And I have changed a lot since I wrote the first edition of this book.

I've often wondered what it would be like to have a conversation with a younger me. What if I could warp time, go back twenty years, and sit down in my old pastor's office with the person I was back then.

Would we even like each other? Would we be able to communicate? Would the younger me recognize the current me?

While I was rewriting this book, I had the chance to experience a bit of that sort of time warp. Much of this material was originally published in 1991 in a book called *The Vineyard*. That book was republished in a couple of different formats. Some of it was put into a coffee table book titled *In My Father's Vineyard* and some of it was repackaged in a book titled *Tales of the Vine*. Those books have been out of print for some time and many people have been asking if I was going to republish my material on the vineyard. As I started through those books again, I wasn't prepared to meet the Wayne of twenty years ago who wrote and thought very differently from the Wayne I've become in the intervening years.

While still embracing the content of the book I wrote, I had to cringe when I read my own words. They sounded more like the fiery preacher of my former days—the one who talked down to my listeners from a pulpit. I was constantly setting a high bar and pushing them toward it (as if our own human effort could ever bear the fruit of our Father). I hope that now after some reworking, it tenderly encourages you to find Jesus in the reality of your life today and find the grace to follow him as he shapes your life to be fruitful and fulfilled in him.

As I reworked this material, a powerful theme emerged that highlighted the seasonal element of our spiritual journeys. We tend to conform our lives to obligations that do not fit what he is asking of us, instead of appreciating the process of fruitfulness that allows each of us to be free in our journey to follow Jesus as each day requires.

Many believers I know live as though it is always supposed to be harvest time and they grow frustrated when their lives are not as fruitful in other seasons. If harvest is our only expectation, then we'll despise the days when Jesus shapes our lives in the relative stillness of winter, or holds us in his hands while we face the heat of summer, bringing maturity to his fruit in us. Vines are never frustrated with shifting seasons. Each one is essential to the cycle of fruitfulness that God invites us to embrace.

As a farmer's view of John 15, this book touches on the deepest themes that have defined my life, while also drawing from the fondest memories I have of growing up on my father's vineyard in central California. That may sound more spectacular than it was in actuality. Today vineyards are marketed as romantic tourist destinations, but for those who live on them they are a lot of hard work.

During summer it is hot and dusty as the farmer cares for the vines or harvests the crops. In winter the labor can be cold and menial as he prunes one row of vines after another. Nonetheless it was in those fields that my young life was shaped. It was in my father's vineyard that I learned so much about God and life. There I learned the nobility of an honest day's work, of the joy in a job well done, and what character and integrity really mean. All of these lessons have served me well in the forty years since I've left that farm.

It took far longer to rewrite this than I had planned, but I hope the result will set you free to live deeply in the Father's life and flow with his working, whether he is pruning you in the rest of winter or developing fruit in you that he can share with so many others.

Who knows, I may have to rewrite it again in twenty years and take more of the old me out yet again.

Chapter 1

An Amazing Invitation

Remain in me, and I will remain in you.
JOHN 15:4

My dad used to say that most people only get enough of God to be miserable. The longer I live, the more I am convinced he's right.

If you only think of God as a meddlesome deity who demands that you follow his rules to live in his good graces, you're probably one of those people. If the thought of having God with you during the day causes your stomach to churn with feelings of failure and inadequacy, you're probably one of those. And if your Christian experience is nothing more than following a set of rituals, rules, and obligations that you think makes him happy, then you're also probably one of those people.

Most people didn't start out that way. They will tell you of their early days of faith when God first captured their hearts. At the beginning, they knew they were loved and they began each day with fresh excitement and anticipation.

Soon, others began to teach them what it meant to be a good Christian, and they began the long, slow descent into the rules and regulations of a religion called Christianity. The religion eventually erased their joy. They became content merely to plod along, unconsciously becoming obedient to human obligations instead of faithful to Jesus.

This is not the life Jesus offered his followers. On the night before he went to the cross he told them that his desire for them was "my joy might be in them and that their joy might be full." That doesn't sound like laboring under the onerous demands of religious practice. Jesus showed them that his Father was the most endearing personality in the universe and that he loved them more than anyone else on the planet. He invited them into a relationship that would fill them with unknown depths of joy and lead them to completely fulfilled and fruitful lives.

Jesus didn't come to inaugurate a new religion complete with rituals, principles, and obligations that only serve to wear us out. I'm convinced he came for quite the opposite reason. He came to fill up the space in the human spirit that chases after religious ritual in order to satiate guilt. He wanted to set people free. He did not take his disciples to the temple to teach them this lesson. He took them to the vineyard.

What a strange night it had been! As Jesus served the Passover meal he made ominous comments about the bread being his broken body and the wine his spilled blood. He said that before the morning sunrise one of them would betray him, one of them would deny him, and the rest of them would abandon him. He told them not to be afraid and warned them that he was going somewhere they could not go. Judas fled the room for reasons none of them understood. They left the safe confines of that upper room and headed through the darkness into the Garden of Gethsemane. Suddenly Jesus took the conversation in an unforeseen direction.

"I am the true vine."

Eyebrows must have popped up as they looked incredulously at one another. *Vines? Why is he talking about vines?*

Perhaps Jesus had spotted a small stand of vines in the garden. I can imagine him walking over to a grapevine, affectionately taking one of the canes in his hand. He might even have squatted down near its trunk, inviting his disciples to gather around him as he launched into one of the more tender metaphors of his ministry—one he reserved for his closest friends.

He compared himself to a vine, his disciples to branches, and his Father to a gardener. He spoke of the seasons through which his Father would care for them, producing the most amazing fruit. Why was he telling them this story? "I have told you this so that my joy may be in you and that your joy may be complete."

What an unlikely group for such an incredible promise! Take a look at the men sitting around that grapevine. Which of these eleven men deserved it? Four years earlier, which would you have chosen to dine with a king, much less the Creator of the universe?

None of these men had been to state dinners at Herod's palace, and none were likely to be invited to one in the future. They weren't outcasts necessarily, but most were nondescript people who you would pass on the street and not give a second thought to. He found some of them on the docks, frustrated fishermen who had worked all night and come up empty. One he found in a tax office, and another was sitting beneath a fig tree.

Who would have thought such a promise would be given to people such as these? Certainly their friends wouldn't have, or the Pharisees. Cultures only reward a sliver of people they consider special, and it usually comes down to those with the right talents, backgrounds, breaks, or achievements. These men, however, were ordinary people who demonstrated the same weaknesses we do—anger, jealousy, greed, and incredible thick-headedness—and Jesus extended to them the amazing invitation to absolute joy.

He paused in that small vineyard on the way to the olive grove in Gethsemane to teach these men—and through them all of us—how to embrace joy at a far deeper level than their circumstances would ever allow.

Joy is not mere happiness—that temporal feeling of satisfaction resulting only from favorable circumstances. This is a joy that springs from the deepest part of your soul with a knowing that he is with you and his purpose is being fulfilled even in the most difficult times.

Discovering joy is the heart of the lesson of the vineyard. You may seem as unlikely a candidate as the eleven men who surrounded Jesus in that garden, and unless you are convinced that the same offer is yours, you will never pursue it with the fervency necessary to apprehend it.

I've met many people who couldn't imagine that such a treasure could be theirs. Through the hollow glare in their pain-filled eyes they all ask the same questions: "What hope do I have of ever knowing joy? Can God help me find the same fulfillment in Christ that you have?" Some were brought to that point through years of abuse or abandonment, others through the brokenness of sin or after years of disappointed spiritual pursuit.

One such person came to me recently. Everyone who had ever been close to Judy, from her birth parents to her adopted parents, had rejected her. She was a real-life Cinderella, but without the carriage and glass slipper. She believed in God, but believed that God had made her only to help expose the sins of others; her personal pain mattered not a whit to him. She reached this conclusion only after her many pleas for healing had seemingly gone unanswered. Everything she tried had failed, and she was left to the bitter throes of loneliness and bulimia.

Was there hope for her? And just as importantly, is there hope for you? You've tried to find a vital friendship with Jesus any number of times, but your experience, like Judy's, may never have lived up to the promise. Let me assure you at the outset that the promises made in the vineyard are as certain for you as the sun rising tomorrow. God has no favorites; he loves all his children equally. Jesus offered the promise of joy not only to the eleven in the garden that evening, but also to rich young rulers, hardened Pharisees, lonely beggars, and brazen prostitutes. Not all took his offer, but those who did never expressed disappointment.

You need to let go of the past with all its unanswered questions and give yourself a fresh start. It is a process and it will take time as God untwists your distorted thoughts and shines light into your dark places. It will challenge you, but you don't need to shrink back from him in guilt or unworthiness.

His touch is tender and his love is certain. He did not come to condemn you for the places you got stuck, but to rescue you from them and set you in his glory. All you have to do is keep coming to him with the simple request that he reveal himself to you.

There is no brokenness he cannot mend, no pain he cannot heal, and no person he does not invite to the fullness of his life. He desires an intimate friendship with you, and he wants to help you engage in a conversation with him that gives wisdom and comfort to your heart.

That's why he told the story of the vineyard to a group of people about to face the greatest trial of their young lives.

Chapter 2

In My Father's Vineyard

I am the vine; you are the branches.
If a man remains in me and I in him,
he will bear much fruit; apart from me you can do nothing.
JOHN 15:5

I was born into a family of farmers. My father owned and lived on a vineyard, as did his father before him. I grew up among rows of grapevines that stretched toward the horizon. I have worked in the vineyard during the heat of summer and the frigid cold of winter. It was in the vineyard that I began my spiritual journey.

This is why John 15 is one of my favorite passages in Scripture. In it Jesus uses the metaphor of a vineyard to teach his disciples how they could follow him into a relationship with his Father that would make them fruitful and fill them with his own special brand of joy. As a farmer in a vineyard, a student of Scripture, and someone who has been on a life-long adventure of growing to know the Father, I want to invite you into the vineyard with me to learn what so many have missed. Jesus really did offer each one of us a relationship with his Father that is more real than the breath we take and more natural than we dare believe.

My favorite time in the vineyard is the waning days of winter. It is still only mid-February, but in the short winters of California's

San Joaquin Valley, spring is just around the corner. The ever-lengthening days are already clawing at winter's grip.

In the late afternoon the long yellow rays of the setting sun have surrendered to violet-tinted shades of pink. Though it was a warm afternoon, the evening chill comes quickly. I zip up my coat against the light breeze, pulling the collar up around my neck and thrusting my hands into the pockets.

Lights from distant farmhouses have already begun to twinkle against the fading landscape, and out of the diaphanous shroud of evening ground fog that obscures the horizon, rows of grapevines curl over the hills and completely surround me.

The vines are all neatly trimmed, their branches gently twisting around the wire strung from the posts that stand as sentinels beside each vine. The hard work of winter brings surrealistic order to the vineyard. Should anything in God's creation be so tightly clipped and neatly arranged?

The vineyard is at rest, waiting patiently for the glory of springtime and another season of fruitfulness. I guess that's why I like this time of year so much. In the moments just before darkness settles in, the wispy fog and the neatly trimmed rows combine to grant me that marvelous gift of secluded peace. Except for the softened whine of a few cars far away, the only sound I hear is the crunching of dirt clods underfoot.

Only a few months ago the air was filled with dust, voices, and churning of tractor engines that mark the frenzied drive of harvest to get the raisins in before the first rain. A few weeks from now those same noises will fill the air as the process of fruitfulness starts all over again.

But now it is quiet. And though a glance from a distant farmhouse might lead someone to believe that I am alone, it is not so. I have come here at this time to walk and talk with the Father.

This has been my cherished prayer closet since I was a young boy. It is a sanctuary of greater reverence than I've known in any cathedral built by human hands. No place on earth more quickly draws me to him, because it is here that we first met, and here we have met so often. This is where I began my spiritual journey.

This is my father's vineyard—a thirty-five-acre ranch in the heart of California's Central Valley. For almost all of his first sixty-five years he lived and worked within a mile of this very spot. The farthest he ever traveled, interestingly enough, put him in another vineyard, this one in northeastern France, where he was wounded in battle just before New Year's Day 1945.

After the war he purchased the farm next to the one on that he was reared. This vineyard provided for his family, but more importantly, also provided the opportunity to teach his four sons about God and his ways. I've learned more about God in this vineyard than in all my years of Bible training and study.

I learned from the lessons Dad taught us and that he backed up in the integrity of his own life and experience. I learned about the cycles of the seasons, of God's faithfulness, of overcoming adversity, and of surrendering to his will. Most of Dad's lessons came from Scripture, but many others came from his lifetime of growing grapes.

And I grew to know God in my long walks through the vines, usually at dawn or dusk. I read Scriptures and learned to voice my concerns to him, telling him my deepest secrets. Eventually I began to hear him respond—simple stirrings, gentle insights, and eventually deep convictions; the voice of God superimposed over my own thoughts. I could know what was on his heart in the same way I was letting him know what was on mine.

I remember the first time I touched a presence bigger than myself. I wasn't more than eleven or twelve years old and had gone for a long walk. I was standing in a row of vines some distance from the farmhouse and made a simple request. "God, if you're real, would you show yourself to me?"

Honestly, I didn't mean at that exact instant, but in the next moment a soft breeze wafted through the vines. My skin began to vibrate as I sensed something or someone was coming close. I looked about anxiously to see if any of my brothers had followed me out into the vineyard, but they had not. The air became rich and clear and my mind filled with thoughts about the God I'd always wanted to know.

He seemed to surround me and flow right through me. My heart pounded, the hair on my neck stood straight out. At first it was pure delight, but the more I questioned what was happening, the more fearful I became that a voice would speak or a vine would suddenly burst into flames. I wasn't ready for that. Eventually the fear overwhelmed me and I ran back to the farmhouse as fast as I could.

What had I touched? It was a presence undeniably distinct from my own. It felt wonderful and scary all at the same time. And though I promised myself I'd never do that again, I would soon find that my desire for him would overrun my fears and I'd find myself again praying that prayer. He didn't ever show up like that again, but he continued to make himself known to me in ways that endeared my heart to him as I continued to grow.

That's why the vineyard has always been my special place, and it is no wonder to me that when Jesus wanted to reveal the reality of living in his kingdom he made rich use of farming and, in particular, vineyard illustrations. No other metaphor offers such a rich source of instruction, encouragement, and challenge.

The passages of Scripture that deal with vines and grapes are among my favorite. I have not only studied them but also lived them, and they have changed my life. The vineyard of my childhood is not so different from those that Jesus would have walked through with his disciples and spoke of in stories.

On that last night before his impending trial and excruciating execution, he wanted to prepare his disciples for life with him beyond his death and resurrection. Where did he take them? He brought them to a vineyard to teach them their last lesson. Among those vines he spoke of a greater vineyard beyond space and time—his Father's vineyard. He told them that he alone could make them fruitful and in doing so would put his joy in us so that our joy might be full.

Fruitfulness and fulfillment are the themes of the vineyard. Who doesn't want joy and peace deep enough to hold us through the worst circumstances, and a sense of purpose that comes from knowing our lives make a difference in the world?

For many, however, these promises remain only an elusive mirage. Though many things in this world promise fulfillment, they only bring moments of happiness that quickly fade to emptiness. None of them offer the enduring joy and peace we were told they would give us. So people are not surprised when religion's joy seems fleeting as well, when the joy of salvation quickly gives way to the rigors of discipline.

Sadly, most think they are the only ones who feel that way. They look around not knowing that others are pretending as well. Even those Christians who try to convince others that they have found the secrets of fulfillment and fruitfulness often prove by their own personal stress, immorality, or spiritual emptiness that they have not.

Religious activity will never lead to the fruitfulness and fulfillment Jesus promised his followers. When Jesus led them to a vineyard he wanted them to know that the way to the fullness of life lies through the reality of a relationship—not the dictates of a religion.

I have long since left the ranch and moved to more urban settings. My days are no longer filled with vineyards but with computers, automobiles, and other machinery of our technological age. It is easy to be seduced into the mistaken notion that spiritual growth lies in carefully observed principles and rituals, rather than the more organic realities of a growing relationship.

We are organisms, not machines. Our spiritual growth patterns have more in common with the four grapevines growing today in my backyard than they do with the computer on which I am typing. That is why when it comes to spiritual growth, Scripture makes such vivid use of the images of a vine growing in a vineyard and the ever-shifting seasons that influence its growth.

Let's go to the vineyard together, you and I. Let's walk the rows with the Father of the vineyard and watch his vines grow and bear fruit. We'll even get to stop, pull back the leaves, and behold the marvelous process of bringing a vine to fruitfulness. Let him teach you the lessons of the vineyard and show you the secret of finding the fullness of joy and fruitfulness that he promised to every believer—including you!

Chapter 3
The Seasons of the Vineyard

There is a time for everything, and a season
for every activity under heaven:
a time to be born and a time to die,
a time to plant and a time to uproot.

ECCLESIASTES 3:1

Who led you to believe that every day should bring a harvest, or that fruitfulness is borne out of days of great joy and ease?

Those who do not understand the life cycle of a vineyard seek to live in the illusion that all days should be the same, that life should be one continuous harvest, or that a life of blessing is a life free of challenge and pain. They grow easily frustrated when their circumstances don't fit their carefully laid plans, as if God and heaven have conspired against the journey.

But there is no way to comprehend life in a vineyard without an appreciation for the seasons that govern its life and the process God uses to bring a vine to fruitfulness. It takes all four seasons to bring a harvest. One is not more important than the other; each has a purpose in the glorious process. Without the bitter cold of winter, the branch cannot be pruned. Without the hot days of summer, the fruit will not ripen.

My computer works the same whether it's a January morning or a July afternoon. If I type, it responds. But that's not true of the grapevines growing on the hillside beyond my window. For them the seasons make all the difference. Winter gives way to an explosion of spring, spring to the overbearing summer, summer to the gentle autumn, autumn to winter's chill. It has been so since that first dawn and it will continue until the last.

Our globe circles the sun with a spectacular tilt that lets the sun be shared in the course of a year over the widest possible area of the globe. This carefully chosen orbit produces in each hemisphere an unending cycle of seasons. As the sun spreads its beams over the Northern Hemisphere we experience the hot days of summer, while the southern part of our globe endures winter. Our days are longer, theirs shorter. But in June the sun begins its southern retreat. Our days diminish in length as theirs grow. As much as people love the days of summer, winter is no less important to the fruitfulness of the vine.

At every moment, what the farmer does in the vineyard is dependent upon these seasons. If he tries to gather grapes in spring he will find only the smallest beginnings of a harvest yet to come. No one will eat these grapes. If he tries to prune in summer he will only destroy the vine he cares for. The seasons control everything the farmer does in his vineyard.

Anyone who has walked with God for any length of time recognizes that God works with us at different times in different ways. At some moments our lives seem to bubble over with joy and ease. At every turn we see God's hand moving, and when we open the Scriptures the words seem to leap off the page with insight and meaning.

At other times the joy we experience is far deeper as we endure painful or distressing circumstances. During such times recognizing God's voice is not easy. Needs press us from all sides. We may find ourselves repenting far more often than rejoicing. If we don't understand God's working in seasons, we'll make the mistake of assuming that the moments of euphoria are what Christianity is meant to be, and anything less is proof of his displeasure.

Look at the life of Jesus. His life was marked by seasons when he was overjoyed and by those when he was deeply troubled, only able to offer up "prayers and petitions with loud cries and tears." We see him in crowded moments with great numbers of people clamoring for his attention, and at others alone on the hillside taking time to be alone with his Father. We see him making wine for a young couple's wedding, and later driving out moneychangers from the temple.

Jesus was not afraid to embrace the changing spiritual seasons of his life and those around him. He didn't follow a rigid code that could direct him through every circumstance he faced. Rather, he flowed with whatever he saw his Father doing, responsive in each moment to his purpose in ever-changing situations.

We would do well to follow his lead. Our spiritual growth demands an ever-changing climate where God's work is tailor-made to our present circumstances. The sun does not control these seasons. They are controlled by the Father as he spurs us toward fruitfulness. These seasons will bring us a healthy balance of both joyful and challenging moments, of diligent effort and renewing rest.

Each season offers something that the vine needs for its continued growth. Spring brings the needed rain and softened days to help stimulate growth without crushing it in the searing heat. Summer offers enough sun to bring the grapes to maturity. Autumn offers the opportunity for harvest undaunted by rain and a chance for the vine to restore itself before winter. Finally, winter brings a much-needed rest and the opportunity to restage the vine for a new season of fruitfulness. Without these changing seasons there would be no fruit.

The same is true for our spiritual journeys. Fruitfulness emerges out of God's process to shape our lives for his purpose through our daily struggles. We aren't always meant to live in the joy of harvest. Fruit matures in the difficult days of challenge and perseverance. If we don't understand these shifting seasons we'll find ourselves fighting God's work instead of embracing it.

Faulty religion teaches people that their efforts can induce God to fill their lives with comfort and favor. If we do good, pray the right way, or work the disciplines hard enough we can get God to do what we want. Without saying it overtly, religion seeks to teach people that they can manipulate God to do their will. Those who believe this lie end up in despair when their circumstances don't change the way they want. They think either God is failing them or that they just can't do what it takes to please him.

To engage God's process of fruitfulness we should spend far less effort trying to change our circumstances; and thus we will find far more freedom in learning to respond to God as we go through them. What he shapes in us becomes far more important than our own comfort. Each season we will receive something needed for continued growth. If we could remain in any one season continually fruit would never grow. By responding to God in whatever season we're in, we can embrace his work and we can let go of even those things we love when the seasons shift. All of it is part of making us fruitful.

We can enjoy the benefits each season brings and also endure in the challenges for the greater work in our lives. And each has its challenges. The dangers brought on by weeds and invading insects can be overcome, but they cannot be resisted. Without the pruning of winter and the discipline of spring, nothing will grow. The same is true of the long, hot days of summer that ripen the fruit.

Jesus' example on the cross teaches us that life can be celebrated in the midst of pain. Not all suffering is harmful. It can produce the very fruit that brings great pleasure to the Father. Though he never delights in those things that hurt us, he does realize how necessary some of them are to bring us into the fullness of his glory.

We will begin our journey in spring and continue to walk through the vineyard in its various seasons. As we see what the vine is going through, we'll look for parallels in our spiritual lives. Seeing God's hand through these moments will leave us more equipped to recognize his working in us and less anxious trying to get God to change our circumstances to make us more comfortable.

As we begin however, let me highlight one important distinction between seasons in the vineyard and seasons in our lives. In the vineyard, all vines endure the same climatic realities together. They are all pruned in the winter, cultivated in the spring and summer, and harvested in the fall.

You will soon discover that this is not true of our spiritual lives. God deals with each branch on the vine individually, giving special care to its own unique growth. And since our seasons are not controlled by external elements of our environment, they may not line up with anyone else around us. I may be enduring the restaging of winter while someone near me is enjoying the fun of harvest.

That is why Scripture warns us repeatedly not to compare ourselves to others, and why when we do, we end up confused (2 Corinthians 10:12). Often when we compare ourselves with someone else, we compare the best thing going on in his life with the worst going on in ours. Instead of looking at the rest and refreshment that God brings through my spiritual winter, I instead focus on the circumstances that surround it: diminished activity and fresh wounds from the recent pruning. When looking at the person who is in the middle of a fruitful harvest, I highlight their joy and acclaim, and forget the risk and cutting that go on in those days as well. What is even more ironic in this scenario is that while a wintering branch may covet the harvest, the branches in the busyness of harvest will long for the peace and serenity of winter!

All of God's branches would be far better served if they stopped looking around for something better and instead embraced the present work of God.

God is always working. Jesus assured us of that (John 5:17). It may not seem like it sometimes, since we may have missed his hand in the distractions or challenges we're facing, or because he isn't doing what we think he should be doing. Instead of comparing or complaining, I am better off looking for the way God is working in my life at that moment. That's the key to walking with God.

He determines the seasons of our lives, such as when to prune, when to feed, or when to harvest our fruit. We are his followers, and he wants to teach you how to follow him.

Spring
New Life Begins

*See! The winter is past; the rains are over and gone
Flowers appear on the earth; the season of singing has come,
the cooing of doves is heard in our land.
The fig tree forms its early fruit;
the blossoming vines spread their fragrance.
Arise, come, my darling; my beautiful one, come with me.*

SONG OF SONGS 2:11–13

Springtime in the vineyard is filled with the hope and promise as the new shoots burst from the vine and stretch toward the warming sun as it arcs above the vines and beckons them to a new cycle of fruitfulness.

Chapter 4

Hope Springs Eternal

Let us hold unswervingly to the hope we profess,
for he who promised is faithful.
HEBREWS 10:23

Slowly at first, and almost imperceptibly, the branches stir to life. The warming afternoon air signals the end of winter. The vine responds with a flow of sap that moves up through the vine and into the branches. Tiny drops of sap glisten at the end of the freshly pruned canes and the buds begin to swell, but there is no other sign of life.

On the farm the vines are not the first to signal the return of spring. The white blossoms of the almond tree and the vivid pink of the peaches break out much earlier. The vine takes its time, not willing to send out its tender leaves until the dangers of frost have passed.

Then one day, as if on cue, the buds of the vine open and, looking down the vineyard row, one can see the faintest tint of green. The tiny leaves curl out of the opening bud and aim skyward. These tender shoots are an iridescent green, almost transparent against the low-lying sunbeams of dawn. They are soft and pliable. In ensuing days, watered by the spring rains and coaxed out by the ever-warming sun, the growth is rapid as a bright green laurel crowns the row of grapevines. Every leaf is fresh and clean, spreading out to catch the sunshine. Underneath them the blossoms emerge, promising a future day of harvest months away.

The fruitfulness of the vine begins in the earliest days of spring and so it is with our spiritual journeys as well. This is where fruitfulness begins in a season where love, joy, beauty, and promise fill our lives. This is where God's love overwhelms us with joy, where we seem to touch his presence at every turn, and where our heart easily delights in the joy of knowing him.

We sense his voice with remarkable clarity and find no circumstance greater than our faith, especially since so little challenges us in this season. We are filled with hope and promise for days to come and blossom with confidence in God's ability to bring our hopes to pass. Following on the heels of the colder and more difficult days of winter, spring is always welcome. Each day offers a fresh adventure in God's grace.

This is the time when our connection with the vine is firmly established. He is the vine; we are the branches. Our life comes from him, and moments of peace are the best time to cultivate that friendship. Most, however, are content to coast along in the ease of spring and miss the opportunity to deepen their friendship with him. There are many who have started down this journey and somehow got lost when circumstances turned painful. Growing doubts, an unkind word from a friend, or even an unhealthy preoccupation with the things of this world slowly turned their hearts away from him toward more temporal comforts.

Spring is the best time to get acquainted with Jesus so that our connection to him deepens. We will need that far more in the days to come than we do when our lives feel so full. It is also the best time to learn to follow his voice and learn the ways he works in our lives.

If not, we'll look back months later at the nostalgia of these days of promise with the frustration of aborted hopes. We'll mistakenly wonder why we didn't try hard enough or blame God for withdrawing from us. We never realize that we were the ones who didn't take the time, when we had it, to get to know him and learn how to rely on his love.

Chapter 5
A Father You Can Trust

I am the true vine, and my Father is the gardener.
JOHN 15:1

My Father is the Gardener, Jesus told his followers that night. While Jesus is the vine, his Father is the master of the vineyard. Depending on how you view God, this can be great news or bad news.

Unfortunately many people come to salvation because they fear the consequences of not doing so. For them God is not an endearing personality in the creation, but a terrifying judge, offended by sin and ready to lash out at those who don't do things his way. They believe his lordship of the vineyard is nothing more than "might makes right."

For people who have been schooled in this fear, having God as the superintending presence in the vineyard does not set their hearts at rest. They may not realize that their fear and the anxiety of displeasing him will abort the process of fruitfulness. Such thoughts are particularly common to people who have felt powerless in the face of someone else's demands on their life. School bullies and, more painfully, domineering fathers and authority figures, teach this lesson all too well: They take advantage of people for their own gain and discard them when they can no longer be exploited.

"Might makes right" to the abused means that the strong get their way because everyone else is helpless against them.

No mind-set could be more wrong when directed toward the Master of the vineyard.

I know a young couple who have a chronically ill child. They may never see him grow to adulthood. Despite their earnest pleadings, God has not yet done one visible thing to improve the health of their child. Day after day they watch him suffer in pain, waiting for what they perceive to be his impending death and confused about God's intentions for them.

I hurt every time I pray for them because in my own limited way I understand their feelings. Our own firstborn child had a severe case of jaundice. Every day we bundled up our fragile infant against winter's penetrating cold and took her back to the hospital, where they drew blood from her tender feet. Our days-old daughter screamed in pain.

We watched those first five days as her blood count continued to climb. The doctor told us that if the count didn't drop, we would have to put her back in the hospital. Even though her condition wasn't life threatening and her pain relatively minimal, I remember how frustrated I was driving back from the hospital that afternoon wondering why we couldn't just take our daughter home and enjoy her like everyone else.

When I think of this young couple, and multiply my five-day frustration by eight years, I begin to get a glimpse into their distress. To them, hearing that God needs to be trusted because he is bigger than anyone else may not be all that comforting.

If we see him as the Landowner of the vineyard, we can understand God's authority and our accountability to him. He is God, after all, and we expect no less. To stop there, however, will lead us to a severely distorted picture of God. We not only need to see the authority he holds, but how he exercises that authority.

Isaiah paints a touching portrait of God caring for his vineyard with great compassion. He watches over it. He waters it continually.

He guards it day and night so no one can harm it. What Jesus wanted his followers to understand more than anything else was that his Father loves them more than anyone else could. This is the growing confidence out of which fulfillment and fruitfulness arise.

The word translated *gardener* or *husbandman* in John 15 carries the meaning of one intimately involved in the growth and nurturing of the vines. This, Jesus said, depicts the Father's role in the garden. He is not just the awesome majestic Creator of all, he is also a God of gentle tenderness who treats the objects of his creation with overwhelming love. The picture of the vineyard draws together both aspects of God's nature and presents them to us in a dynamic tension that makes God wholly attractive. He cares for each branch with intimate care.

I have seen the reflection of that care in my earthly father's eyes toward his own vineyard. He was part of a passing generation of family farmers. He cared for his own vines, refusing to buy more land than he could farm himself. He could never have been a manager of a farming conglomerate. If you were to pass by his farm, he (or his children) would be out in the morning frost pruning the vines or driving the tractor through a moving cloud of dust.

He retired and sold his farm because he would not stay on the land beyond his ability to farm it. Many farmers hire out the work to others, or even rent out the entire vineyard to someone else's care. They still live on the farm, but only as landlords. Not my father. He did not relish hired hands in his vineyard. He only hired others for the work he could not possibly do himself, and that with great apprehension.

No one he ever hired met his exacting standards. That wasn't because he thought of himself as the world's greatest farmer. He knew that no one else would care for his vineyard as much as he did. When he did have to hire out, he preferred his family and friends who would most closely share his concern.

I've seen the disappointed look in his eye when he saw raisins carelessly strewn on the ground after someone had turned the trays or rolled them. The person paid by the number of trays doesn't care whether a bunch falls off or not. His wages will be adversely affected if he stops his momentum to pick it up.

I've also felt his pain when he gazed at a vine I carelessly pruned. In my haste to race my brothers to the end of the row, I had cut off too many good canes. There were not enough left for the vine to reach its full potential in the year ahead. I remember my father's patience in telling us to slow down, training us to do a better job.

But no lesson was more powerful than the fact that I had let him down. My treatment of that vine hurt him. I could see it in his eyes, even though he demonstrated no anger. I looked at the good canes laying useless on the ground at my feet. *If only I could glue them back on . . .*

Earlier, Jesus had illustrated his care for each of his followers with a different metaphor. Perhaps he knew that we could understand care directed to animals more easily than grapevines. If you've ever had a pet you deeply loved, you'll understand a shepherd's love for his sheep.

> *I am the good shepherd. The good shepherd lays down his life for the sheep. The hired hand is not the shepherd who owns the sheep. So when he sees the wolf coming, he abandons the sheep and runs away. Then the wolf attacks the flock and scatters it. The man runs away because he is a hired hand and cares nothing for the sheep.*
>
> —JOHN 10:11–13

Here's an interesting shepherd. In the midst of danger he willingly lays down his life for the sheep, risking his own to keep them safe. That's how deeply Christ loves his own. No hired hand would show the same care; he will labor only until the pain or risk exceeds the quantity of his paycheck—then he's off to find safer pastures.

How could anyone think to risk a human life for a sheep? How about a God who would trade his life for yours? This is the gardener who planted you in his vineyard. His vine is his own Son, and each branch another son or daughter. He loves them more than any other ever could.

I can't explain to the young couple why their son suffers so; though I understand their pain, it is truly misdirected if they think the Father is the source of it. He loves them and their son, and though I can't explain why he hasn't healed him from this, I know God is not to blame for his suffering.

God has not hung back indifferent to their prayers or to their pain, but has labored over the suffering as well. He wants to redeem their situation, bringing glory out of pain. But in order to see it they will have to let go of their mistaken conclusions and trust him. Disappointment and hurt can be difficult obstacles to overcome, but the Father knows that. That's why he comes to us with such tenderness.

The gardener is fully capable of taking any branch, no matter how broken, and putting it back together again. This may not mean a quick fix. It may take a while, but the Father has grace enough to forgive our failures, strength enough to transform any crises into something for his glory.

Even when others worked for my father, he kept a sharp eye on their work. Long after they had gone home to rest for the day, my father would walk the rows after them. He was always the last one to leave the vineyard. He would pick grapes that had been missed, scoop up raisins that had been spilled in the dirt, and rewrap canes on the wire that had been done carelessly.

I have seen God do the same thing in the lives of his people. No matter what we endure, no matter how much others might have failed us, he wants to be the last one to touch every area of our lives. He will clean up our mistakes and the damage caused by the abuses of others, and he will bring fruitfulness out of the direst circumstance.

The story of Joseph is not unique in the Father's vineyard—it reveals his heart for all of his children. The envy of Joseph's brothers led him to be sold as a slave in Egypt. There we still find God, working to fulfill his plan for Joseph even though others meant him great harm. Later, when Joseph was falsely accused because of the integrity of his heart, God used his unjust jail sentence as a stepping-stone to the highest rank in Pharaoh's kingdom.

Can you believe him to do the same in your own life? If you are looking to the Father, he will heal your hurts and override your failures, using both as stepping-stones to growth.

Now that's good news!

Chapter 6
I've Been Chosen

*You did not choose me, but I chose you and appointed you
to go and bear fruit—fruit that will last.*

JOHN 15:16

Anyone who has ever waited to be the last chosen for a team in grammar school knows the terrifying humiliation of not being wanted.

Regrettably, many of us carry that same feeling into our relationship with God. "Whosoever will" has come to mean that God has to take everybody who comes . . . so when God says, "You are a chosen people, a royal priesthood, a holy nation, a people belonging to God . . ." it doesn't mean anything to us. Yet there is no greater assurance than knowing that Jesus has chosen us to be planted in him.

"I chose you." It was that simple. The twelve had not come to him by their own determination or because they just happened to be at the right place at the right time. Their participation in his life was not a lucky break. He had chosen them.

I wonder how much those words meant to Peter on that treacherous night. Circumstances were tumbling downhill with increasing velocity. Danger and confusion swirled in the darkness. He must have thought, *How did I get myself into this?*

"I chose you." The words must have leaped out at him. How vividly that day was seared in Peter's memory. Exhausted from a long and unsuccessful night at sea, he had just finished cleaning the nets when Jesus approached him. What Peter knew about Jesus before that moment is unclear. We do know that even after his discouraging night of fishing, he consented to Jesus' request to use his boat to speak to the crowd.

Evidently impressed to some degree, Peter called Jesus "Master" shortly after he was finished, and he even agreed to another odd request from Jesus. Yes, he'd put the nets out again—even though they caught nothing the night before and the nets were perhaps already cleaned and folded for another night's work.

He had hardly slipped them overboard when the water began to boil with fish leaping into his net. The load was too big for one man, and he called for help. Though Peter's eyes may have been on the net, his heart was fixed on this incredible man. "Go away from me, Lord; I am a sinful man."

Jesus didn't honor Peter's request, but instead invited him to go fishing again—with him—for people. That was all it took. Peter left his boat and the greatest catch of his life to go on an adventure he couldn't possibly have understood.

I've met two kinds of people who are disappointed by the lack of reality they have found in their relationships with the Savior. The first are those who blame God for not caring enough to help them. Peter is an example of the second type—those who feel like damaged goods. They are too filthy and too ugly to tolerate God's presence. They will tell him to leave them alone, and if he doesn't they'll run away.

But Peter had been chosen, and by that simple act his fears were dispelled. Here is an amazing attribute of this vine: Jesus chooses the branches that will draw life from him. This was not Peter's doing. He had not earned it.

What a difference from anything else in his (and our own) culture. "If you want something, go out and get it. No one is going to walk up and hand it over to you." This is especially true of religion. The religious leaders were a select class; they had to have money or connections to get to the top of the ladder. But in one moment on a makeshift dock Jesus short-circuited the process. Reaching past those who had completed the religious obstacle course of the day, he simply chose Peter. "I want you; will you come?"

Jesus gives us the same invitation because branches in his vineyard don't grow naturally out of his vine, like they did in my father's field. Jesus' words hearken back to a far more special process called *grafting*.

The most detailed picture of how grafting works is painted by Paul in Romans 11:17–24. Though he writes of olive trees, the same process was also used in vineyards. And though he writes in generalities of the Jewish and Gentile nations, he illustrates what we all go through on a personal level so that we can partake of God's life.

Grafting is a nearly miraculous process in which one new plant is made out of two. There are various methods for doing this, but all involve a branch cut from one vine and inserted into a cut on another vine. The two are then bound together with an adhesive compound or tape (or in ancient days mud or clay). As the wound heals, the two plants become one and the new branch draws sap from the roots of the established vine.

Notice that grafting demands a wound in both parties. Jesus, as our vine, was cut open on the cross to make room for us. For us to be grafted into him we must also be wounded in complementary fashion so that we will fit into the place prepared. That's why we have to identify with the death of Christ and die to whatever we were before coming to him. Unless we are cut away from our roots in the past we cannot be placed in him.

The only way we can be grafted is by believing that he chose us. Believing in Jesus means that we will surrender our life to his control and grow in a trusting relationship with him. This reaches to the very heart of Paul's analogy. He points out that grafting is "contrary to nature" and as such superbly illustrates our new life. We can no longer trust the natural ways of our flesh since we've become part of something so wonderfully new.

The reason it is so important for us to know who chose whom at the outset is not only because of the confidence it gives us to pursue Jesus with hope and joy, but also because it sets a serious precedent for everything about the Father's vineyard. Everything the branches need flows through the vine. Moisture and nutrients from the soil are delivered to the branches on the vine's timetable. As that vine, Jesus sets the direction for our lives. He chooses my portion today, my purpose, my feeding. I am to become dependent upon him, a responder in the life of the kingdom, not an initiator. Nothing happens by my choice unless it was first his.

Grafting is a process that can only be done one branch at a time. It requires the personal attention of the gardener as he cuts and fits us into Christ, and a personal response from us. Each of us must respond to him personally. God has no second-generation disciples.

My wife Sara and I were blessed to watch this process in our daughter when she was around twelve. We actively helped Julie develop her own relationship with God that did not run through us. On her twelfth birthday we told her we would be releasing an increasing number of decisions into her hand so that we could help her through the process of learning to hear and believe God's voice.

And it paid off. She was invited to a birthday party of a good friend. This was to be a sleepover event, and since this friend lived out of town, Julie would be the only one not from her friend's school. She had attended daytime parties for this girl and had always felt left out because all the other girls were such good friends.

"Do I have to go, Dad?" she asked with an anguished whine. She knew from plenty of past times that we made her go to the parties of children whom she had invited to her own. "Julie, you're twelve now and the decision is yours. I'm not going to make you go. You need to decide for yourself what is right to do."

Immediately her countenance changed. "Should I go?" the whine was now gone. I wasn't going to make her go and by that simple act I had become someone who could now help her with the decision.

"She came to your last party."

"I know, but Dad, everyone leaves me out." The whine had returned.

"I'm not saying you have to go. I'm only helping you see what to consider. Have you prayed about it yet?" This time I got a scrunched-up nose and that look of "whatever for?"

"Why don't you go up to your room and ask God what he wants you to do? If he wants you to go, then go. If not, then don't."

Twenty minutes later she came back out on the landing. "I'm going to go to the party," she said with a broad smile. It's so much harder to be accountable to God than it is to manipulate a parent, but so much more joyful.

It was a small matter, but my relationship with my daughter had begun to change. God now held the place I had had in her life for her first years. Julie has a heart for God and a desire to please him, and I needed to release her to be grafted into that vine as well. Without being personally grafted in, our life in God will always be empty and irrelevant. We cannot afford to let a parent, pastor, or author get between Jesus and us.

Jesus continues to choose his followers today. He is the one who guarantees our place alongside him. He wants *us*, not our abilities or talents. Whatever excuses we think might prevent that grafting must dissolve along with Peter's, because it was Jesus' choice before it was ever ours.

What is especially magnificent about the Lord's choosing is that his choosing me does not exclude anyone else. When five people compete for a new position in the company, the joy of the person selected is purchased at the severe disappointment of the other four. In the Father's vineyard, however, there is a time (even numerous times) in every life when God extends his hand to choose each person. Not all walk over to join his team, however. Many walk away, unwilling to give up their life to gain his.

No matter how unloved I've felt in the past, no matter how filthy I feel in my sin, God knew who I was when he chose me to be on his team. He wanted me, and he also wants you. Hope for finding fulfillment in his kingdom springs from that simple truth.

I don't know if this was a source of comfort to Peter the morning after he denied Jesus. Jesus knew well how weak Peter's flesh would be in this trial. Yet to him and the others he still said, "I choose you."

And if he has chosen you, what else matters?

Chapter 7

You Are Already Clean

You are already clean because of the word I have spoken to you.
JOHN 15:3

Bear fruit or burn.

That seemed to be the gist of his ominous words: Unless you bear fruit, the Gardener will cut you off and throw you into the fire. But Jesus quickly made clear his words were not a threat.

They, like us, must have wondered where they fit in. What does he think of me? Am I about to be cut off? So just as quickly Jesus made clear how he viewed them: *You are already clean!* Don't worry about the pruner's shears; it is not time for that. You are already neatly trimmed and fit for the season ahead. His invitation to follow him made them clean.

This was not something they had achieved, but a gift they had been given. He wanted them to know this was the Father's passion and that *his* work would get them there, not their own ability or diligence. With all their foibles and fears, with all they didn't understand and their limited spiritual stamina, he saw them as clean. He'd made them that way with his own word. They truly had nothing to fear.

When Jesus told his first followers about his desire to fill them with his joy and to make them fruitful in the world, he invited them into spiritual spring. Nothing is cleaner than when it is new, and that is especially true in the San Joaquin Valley of California. This is a desert, though not one filled with cactus. Left to itself our ten inches of rain a year would produce only brief scrub brush that would swiftly melt into the dust that is such a staple in our valley. Between May and October virtually no rain falls.

Nothing of value would grow if it were not for the abundant aquifer beneath the ground and the yearly runoff from the abundant snow of the magnificent Sierra Nevada mountains to the east. These two resources have turned this desert into a garden, one of the most productive regions on the earth. But even that doesn't eliminate all the dirt. Whenever the fields dry up for even a few days, the ever-present dust returns. It clings to the leaves and is stirred by the slightest movement. Plowing on a tractor, especially downwind, can keep you in a cloud of gagging dust all day long. Even in sealed-up homes, dust is the constant challenge of any homemaker. It is everywhere.

Spring is the one time, however, when the vineyard is absolutely clean. The labor of winter has left the vineyard neatly trimmed and perfectly tied to the long, straight rows of glistening wire. The field is freshly plowed and every weed is shoveled away from the vines. The flexible new canes and miniature leaves are a vivid light green, and spotless. The spring rains have kept the dust at bay.

All is under control. The farmer looks across his vineyard with a deep satisfaction at its beauty and order. Everything is fresh, ready for the fruitful season ahead.

That's where Jesus' followers stood that evening. He had made them clean. Maybe the word pristine is even better. They were not perfect, nor had they matured. Peter would still deny him a few hours later. There was still so much for them to learn about the kingdom Jesus had laid at their feet. As they stood between two worlds—the natural one in which they had become so comfortable and a spiritual world that was opening before their eyes—he made them clean and innocent, ready for what the coming days would unfold.

That's how everyone starts his or her spiritual journey. Jesus finds us and makes us fit and ready. He breathes new life into us and the old creation gives way to the new.

Though we miss it in our translations, Jesus' pronouncement is an interesting word play. The word he uses for "clean" comes from the same root as the word he used for pruning in the sentence before. He demonstrates by his usage exactly what pruning is meant to accomplish: It makes the vine clean in the fullest sense of the word, not just dust-free, but trimmed and ready for growth. Jesus doesn't seem to indicate that they had been freshly pruned. No, in their spiritual life this was their *first* spring. And even though the theme of John 15 is a call to bear fruit, Jesus wasn't asking that of them yet.

This was spring, *not* harvest. They were ready for the process of fruitfulness to begin. Growth in God's kingdom does not aim ultimately for cleanliness; it simply begins there. Jesus' word itself makes us clean and able to stand before God beautifully adorned and blameless. There is no more foundational work than this for bearing fruit. Since fruitfulness arises only out of the depths of our friendship with Jesus, it cannot begin until we are comfortable in his presence, confident that we belong there.

Jesus made a way for us to come to the Father as freshly cleaned as a spring vine. The same word that Jesus used for clean, the writer of Hebrews takes up when he talks about the cleansed conscience of a believer under the New Covenant. Our conscience is made perfect by the work of Christ. It is not an assumption of forgiveness by someone who has traversed the proper theological steps. It is a deep inner conviction that in spite of our weaknesses and failures we are safe with him.

That was the limitation of the sacrifices, which the Old Covenant provided. One had to believe in his forgiveness because he had made a sacrifice. But his consciousness of sin did not depart. From one who seemed to know the difference firsthand, having served God under both covenants, the writer of Hebrews extols the marvelous cleansing of the New Covenant that leads us to God's presence with a perfect conscience. No pang of guilt endures, no fear of punishment remains. His word of forgiveness buries the past at the foot of the cross, removing all stains of sin and rebellion.

We are exhorted to come to God's presence with confidence and boldness; we belong there. Intimacy demands that kind of confidence. Only when atonement is made can friendship ensue. All we have to do to embrace this cleansing is to repent—to turn from living life our own way and choose to live in his. This is the door into his cleansing. Its true the first time we come to know him and every day we walk with him.

God's first priority is not to clean up our sins; it is to help us learn how to live in his love. His cleansing makes that possible even where we still feel entangled in sin. Certainly he wants the cleansing within to untwist our self-indulgent ways, but that only happens as the fruit of living loved. Because we are clean we can live in him. As we live in him his fruit grows in us to displace the waywardness of our old ways.

The Old Testament left us with the impression that the more righteous we could be, the more access we would have to God. But that never worked. Our best efforts still left us woefully short of holiness. Jesus made it clear that relationship with him is the only doorway into righteousness. The more relationship we have with him, the more righteous he will make us.

That's why cleanliness begins the journey. By making us clean we can be joined to him and as his love begins to flow through us he will make the changes in our life that lead us away from the tyranny of self to a fulfilled life in him. But we cannot live in the reality of his love and not find that our self-indulgent thinking begins to yield to that love. The more he untwists us the freer we will become from sin.

Those who come from abused or neglected childhoods or have indulged in sinful lifestyles need to hear this. These circumstances give the enemy an opportunity to plant patterns of thinking that will, if not dealt with, leave you feeling like a second-class citizen in God's vineyard. Don't ever settle there. God wants to heal all the wounds of your past so that you can go on to know the full joy of his kingdom. If you still feel stained by your past, let God deal with it. Seek out the prayer and counsel of others who can help you fully embrace the cleansing that God has already given you.

You'll know this is accomplished when you can rise each day confident that God has great affection for you. Then for the rest of your life guard that cleanliness. Keep it fresh by continued repentance and surrender to God. Don't get defensive at the things God might expose in you, for he only wants to forgive and transform you.

Like the disciples, our first days of faith are our first spring. Nothing better describes those who embark on a new walk in Christ! We begin in his kingdom newly made, fresh and clean. But this is not our only spring in the kingdom. Periodically we will note times when God freshens his presence and renews us with promise and vision. These times will come on the heels of our spiritual winter, when our lives are pruned and prepared for the next work that God wants to do.

Fruitfulness begins in the confidence that he has made us clean. It begins when we can be at rest in the presence of the Holy God, even though our lives don't yet reflect that holiness. That will come in time. For now, we can simply live in the confidence of his love for us and watch what he will do to transform our lives.

Chapter 8
Training the New Vine

Every branch that does bear fruit he prunes
so that it will be even more fruitful.
JOHN 15:2

They're called suckers, and that aptly describes what they do.
They are new canes that sprout from the base of a vine. If left there,
they would suck life out of the vine that would otherwise be directed
into the fruit.

New growth in spring is extremely prolific. Not all of this growth
is good. Too many canes will siphon off the strength of the vine. One
of the most important tasks the farmer accomplishes in the spring is
to direct the growth of the vine so that it will be fruitful.

Suckers, for instance, need to be pulled off. Sometimes at the
beginning even grape bunches are plucked off, either because the crop
is too large or to make sure that the grapes that do mature are larger
and sweeter. Some table-grape farmers girdle their vines, cutting a
trough around the trunk itself, which directs more nutrients to the
grape bunches.

The best place to see the farmer train his vines is with those vines
just entering their first growing seasons. How these new vines are
trained will impact the vine years down the road. The farmer tears off
every shoot that grows from the new vine until it reaches the height

he wants. What the farmer wants is for the young vine to have only one long branch. This will divert all the energy to strengthen that part of the vine, which will help it mature faster and bear fruit sooner.

As it grows taller the farmer clips off the branch at the height he wants the vine to be, in order to allow the shoots to branch off from the top. Branches lower down on the trunk will again be plucked off to force the strength of the vine into the branches that will ultimately bear fruit. Every year after that the farmer has to cut off those branches that grow too low on the vine.

There is no better picture of the Father's discipline in our lives.

Many think of discipline as punishment but it is not. Punishment is retribution, it attempts to control someone's behavior by offering even worse consequences. The Lord's discipline, however, is not to punish us but to train us so that we can grow and produce fruit. This is what the writer of Hebrews had in mind when he wrote, *No discipline seems pleasant at the time, but painful. Later on, however, it produces a harvest of righteousness and peace for those who have been trained by it.* (Hebrews 12:11)

That's why God disciplines those he loves. He wants to bring us to his fullness so that fruit can form in our lives. But, with young growth especially, this is a gentle process. The new growth is so fragile that if the farmer tried to force it, it would easily break. I'm sure that it is uncomfortable, or even painful, for the vine.

We are told to consider any hardship as discipline because he uses these moments to expose the waywardness of our natural ways and to draw us closer to Jesus.

We often resist discipline. We think the path with the least resistance is the best. We rationalize that any restriction in our lives must be legalism, because he wants us to be free! But if you let the branches of a vine grow however they want, they will not be fruitful. They will sprawl everywhere, loaded with leaves . . . but there will be no overflow of strength to sustain growing fruit.

Legalism is when we strive to meet man-made rules or expectations, or when we attempt to *achieve* acceptance and status from God through our works. God has freed us from that. Discipline, however, is responding to God's inner leading as he directs our growth. Obedience is not legalism, nor is it an option if we want to be fruitful. Jesus told his followers that if we're not ready to obey him, we cannot live in his love. That doesn't mean he will not love us if we don't obey, but we cannot live in the reality of his love for us by continuing to go our own way.

Our freedom in Christ is the freedom to follow him. It is not the freedom to do whatever we want. The master of the vineyard prunes and shapes the vine to narrow the flow of sap into a few good branches to insure that it will be fruitful. By learning to follow his will instead of our own, we allow his Spirit to bring us to fruitfulness and fulfillment in God's kingdom.

On the other hand, if we resist God, we will continually be frustrated that the promises he made to us are never fulfilled. Far too many of us have found a niche beneath God's promises. We live to our own comfort or ease in the short-term and then wonder why we never seem to be fruitful in the long-term. Fruitfulness requires intentional action that will often take us beyond our comfort zone.

The best time for discipline is before we need it. The tender shoots of a young vine can be plucked off or tied up to the vine with minimal effort. At this stage the shoots are as flexible as boiled spaghetti. The longer they grow, however, the more rigid they become. Within a year they will break if bent too far. A young vine can be trained to grow straight up the pole if it is carefully tied as it grows.

Learn to listen to God's gentle nudgings on your heart. It is easier to learn to follow him in the early days before we grow rigid over time and blind ourselves to his working. That's also why the first few months of our life of faith can be so crucial. Charles Finney observed that most converts live for a lifetime on the patterns and doctrines they learned within the first three months of their conversion. He saw it as the key time for training, since this is when people are most pliable and receptive. Too many people are rigidly committed to the false or incomplete perceptions of following Christ that they picked up during their first spring.

This is the best season to learn his ways and how to listen to his voice. He can speak through the Scriptures, through a comment from a friend, an event in our lives, or simply by a whisper in our hearts. We learn to recognize his leading through practice.

You will find that the way he thinks and what he wants of you may often run counter to your own wisdom or your personal preference. Like a vine being trained, we prefer to go our own way, and we often misinterpret God's voice to better fit our own ambitions. When we resist God's gentle urgings, he uses our circumstances to bring greater clarity to his voice. Often these are painful because our selfish pursuits and self-sufficiency are revealed for what they are—vain attempts to find life on our own. Consider Psalm 32:8,9:

> *I will instruct you and teach you in the way you should go; I will counsel you and watch over you. Do not be like the horse or the mule, which have no understanding but must be controlled by bit and bridle or they will not come to you.*

God won't have to use the bit and bridle of those painful circumstances when we are willing to respond to the gentle call of his voice. I've seen horses trained well enough that the slightest touch on the side of the neck or a single word from the master is all it needs to perform flawlessly. God desires the same of us.

Learning to follow him means you'll often lay down your life for what he wants and find greater joy in his desires. That's why obedience may seem difficult and risky at the beginning, but in time you'll come to see that his ways are best. Then we will realize at an intuitive level that we are safer in him no matter what our circumstances look like.

As strange as it may sound, growth comes easiest when we are relaxed in him. When life is full, the vine will produce fruit. The process cannot be rushed. Establishing healthy growth is the most important concern of the farmer in those early days. He knows no vine will produce fruit the first year anyway, nor enough in the second and third to make much difference. He is concerned with the vine's fruitfulness and health for the long haul.

That's why the Israelites were told not to eat any fruit the first three years, and set about the fourth year as holy to the Lord: *In this way your harvest will be increased.* (Leviticus 19:23–25). Nothing diminishes the health of a vine more than trying to rush its growth. Learning to live in the love of the Father and follow his voice takes time.

I've seen anxiety in people who are more concerned about overcoming some habit or finding a significant ministry than they are about easing into a relationship with God. I have often told these people they need to be more concerned about coming to know him first. "If you do nothing for two years except learn to listen to him, then it will be time well spent." Some find that advice hopeful and create the space in their life for that relationship to grow. Others brush it off, convinced that their agenda is more important. One path encourages deep growth and a journey that endures for a lifetime; the other is a brief flash in the pan of passion and activity, but soon it whithers into disillusionment.

If you're just starting out, relax into the reality of living loved and learning to listen to his voice. Take your time. He's in no hurry to spur you on to fruitfulness. If you've been one of those who've missed the most important part of this journey because you were too worried about overcoming your sin or seeking a significant place in ministry, it may be time to start fresh.

The Master of this vineyard can take you right back to spring again. He can trim your branch of all the worthless activity and draw you deeply to himself. You will discover that it's fullness in him that makes you fruitful, not fruitfulness that makes you fulfilled.

Chapter 9

Blossoms of Promise

In days to come Jacob will take root,
Israel will bud and blossom
and fill all the world with fruit.

ISAIAH 27:6

Blossoms contain not only some of the most beautiful colors in nature, but many of the most pleasing aromas as well. A peach orchard in bloom is one of the most breathtaking scenes of spring, a brilliant pink cloud suspended above the landscape. The sweet fragrance of an orange grove or lilac trees in blossom overpowers lesser scents and revives the senses.

These floral displays would be treasured if their only purpose were to lend aesthetic beauty to the world. But God made the blossoms of spring for something so much more spectacular: They celebrate the promise of the sweet fruit to come and seeds for a new generation.

The blossoming grapevine is not nearly so spectacular as other plants. Tiny white flowers pop open beneath the leaf cover. You can't even see them from a distance. Neither is their fragrance overpowering. The sweet aroma is subtle and can only be enjoyed if you are trained to notice it. It's no wonder that no one picks grape blossoms for flower arrangements.

For the vineyard, however, they are the glory of spring. It doesn't take a strong vine or even a mature one to bear blossoms. Even the youngest will put forth blooms. Spiritual springtime in our own lives is marked by fresh vision and promise from Jesus himself. At a time when we're exploding with the renewal of his life, he allows us to catch a glimpse of the glory that awaits us.

In inklings that grow ever-clearer in our minds until we can no longer ignore them, God makes his promises to his people: "I want my compassion to fill you so you can help me rescue broken lives." "I've given you a gift of music to break the enemy's hold, just like David's worship soothed Saul." "I'm going to free you from your bondage to other people's expectations." "I'm going to make you as patient as the little brook wearing its way through a huge boulder."

Talk to almost any believer, and in the deepest recesses of his heart you will find that he carries meaningful and significant promises that Jesus breathed into his soul; that is, if he has not already buried them beneath disillusionment and false modesty. Almost always you will find that these promises come in spiritual springtime, when the person's relationship with God is undergoing a season of joyful renewal. God treasures wonderful things in his heart for each of us and discloses them to give us hope and perspective about days to come.

A believer carrying the promise of God on his heart is as beautiful a sight as any plant in bloom. That is, until they lose hope in the promise. Many believers, including some of the most notable men and women in Scripture, thought God's promises would be fulfilled faster than he intended. Grapevines never seem to be in a hurry. They know the fruit will come in its time. We, however, seem to operate on a far faster calendar than our Father does because we are more focused on the fruit than on him who makes the fruit possible.

From a young age I wanted to be a writer. I spent summers writing stories and dreaming of books I'd write. As I got a bit older I began to believe that God wanted my books to have a profound affect on people and concluded I would be an influential and well-known author. Can you imagine my despair when year after year I got rejection notices and even when I got my first book published it didn't sell as well as

I had hoped. It certainly didn't make me the well-known author or generate the income I had hoped for.

When you're focused on the outcome you want, even promises made by God can hang like a lead weight around your neck. After my second book was published, an earlier adaptation of this one, it too couldn't find its way in the marketplace and was soon pulled off the shelves. Shortly after a good friend betrayed me, and all of my dreams blew up in my face, and so, I thought, had God's promises to me.

I grew discouraged in God's promises, even doubting whether he had made them at all. If he had, was he playing some cruel trick? Was he like the father who always promises to spend time with his children but never takes the time away from work to make it happen? Solomon said it best in Proverbs: *Hope deferred makes the heart sick, but a longing fulfilled is a tree of life.*

Had I been mistaken, confusing my own desires for God's promise? In part, yes. God did promise that my writings would touch people, but my own arrogance blew that out of proportion. I was expecting a result that wasn't in his heart. I've had other instances where I have made up promises to fit my own desires.

Rather than be angry at God when things don't turn out the way we hope, it is best to run to him and find out what was truly his promise.

Did I expect fulfillment too soon, and consequently, did I give up too quickly? Our species is an impatient lot. If too many days go by without some physical proof of God's promise, we grow discouraged. I relate well with Habakkuk, the Old Testament prophet of the late sixth century BCE. He offered God two complaints, both dealing with his impatience at God's timing. How did God answer him? *The revelation awaits an appointed time . . . Though it lingers, wait for it; it will certainly come and will not delay.*

We forget that God's promise is proof enough. If we can rejoice and be patient, that blossom will emerge as fully ripened fruit. His promises never fail.

Can his promises go unfulfilled because we didn't follow through on the things he asked of us? While it is God's responsibility to fulfill his promise, we are partners with him in the process. If we ignore his leading when he speaks to us, the plan may not play out as he wanted. And, no, that doesn't mean we have to be perfect for God to fulfill his promise. But if we do not remain in the vine and learn to draw his life, the fruit can whither before it matures.

Many people I deal with carry deep frustrations, if not anger, at God for promises seemingly unfulfilled and needs seemingly unmet. Part of growing in him is taking these real issues to him and finding out what is on his heart. There you can discover what he has really promised you and adjust your course from there. If you've expected him to make your life easy, you'll discover how unrealistic that expectation is.

He doesn't want you to be confused about his promise. The only reason we genuinely make a promise to someone is to set their heart at ease in the present, knowing we will resolve their concerns in the future. His promises are intended to reassure us in our present circumstances, not to add to our frustration or pain.

Scripture is filled with promises so that he can stir hope within us. Faith is the confidence that God will actually do what he promises. If we're certain of his work, we can be at rest—we know we don't have to fulfill the promise in our own strength. This allows us to live free to respond to God's leading instead of inventing schemes to get what he promised. Few of God's promises are arrived at directly. Remember, this is a kingdom where if you try to save your own life you're sure to lose it, and if you want to be first, you'll end up last.

God's promises are actually the means he uses to transform us. The hunger stirred by his promise, our need to learn to trust, and our challenge to follow him instead of relying on our own abilities allows his fruit to grow in our hearts and exposes the corruption of our own desires.

> *Through these he has given us his very great and precious*
> *promises, so that through them you may participate in*
> *the divine nature and escape the corruption in the world*
> *caused by evil desires.* —2 PETER 1:4

Throughout Scripture God made promises to his people and fulfilled them. Through that process he changed his people to be more like him. The father of faith himself, Abraham, is perhaps the best example. God promised to make him the father of a great nation even though he had no children. For twenty-five years Abraham endured that promise, well past the time that he or his wife could ever have had children naturally. Why did God delay? God's promise was to make Abraham the father of a great nation. That meant more than having a child; it meant that he had to be shaped as a man of faith. His promise provided the opportunity for that shaping.

I love the picture Paul paints of this process in Romans 4 as Abraham wrestles with the promise of God to father a great nation. Abraham was far from perfect in this process. Genesis records his failures as well as triumphs—but through them he learned to trust God. That's why Paul made him an example of responding to God's promise with hope, not frustration.

God, who gives life to the dead and calls things that are not as though they were. God called Abraham a father of a great nation before he was even a father. God sees the end from the beginning, and it is precisely this perspective that gives birth to his promises. We can learn to trust God's promises even when there is not a shred of material evidence to validate them.

Abraham in hope believed and so became the father of many nations. Abraham's hope freed God's promise to be fulfilled. If he had given up he still might have had a baby, but he would not have been the example needed to stand as a father of an entire nation.

Without weakening in his faith, he faced the fact that his body was as good as dead since he was about a hundred years old and that Sarah's womb was also dead. Faith never hides from facts. Abraham could look at the tangible evidence without weakening in his faith. Faith that has to hide from reality is not faith at all. But in spite of the lack of material evidence, Abraham had a promise from God. That alone was evidence enough to quell any fear.

Yet he did not waver through unbelief regarding the promise of God, but was strengthened in his faith and gave glory to God. When he brought his disappointing circumstances into his relationship with God, God won out. He could give him glory as that trust deepened.

...being fully persuaded that God had power to do, what he had promised. God is able to do anything, but that doesn't mean he will. The clincher to Abraham's faith was that God would do what he said. It wasn't Abraham's idea to be the father of a great nation. He might have already adjusted to the idea of being childless when God made him the promise. That is why it is so important for us to hear God's voice in our lives. Faith does not rest on God's ability, but on his activity.

The young mother's husband deserted her within a week of the birth of their third child. It was time that she made plans for the future. I was sure that's why she wanted to see me. As we began to talk she told me that she was not concerned, that God had promised her that her husband would return.

I probed her discernment carefully. I have too often seen people cling to their own groundless hope—a made-up promise—as an escape from facing reality. This situation sure looked like that, but something inside told me not to discount it. We talked openly about whether this was God or not, and though I couldn't tell her I heard God confirm it with me, I was convinced of her submission to Jesus. She was not trying to escape.

I encouraged her to stand strong in the promise, open for God to show her differently if she was wrong. Nine months passed and nothing gave us hope of her husband's return. Then out of the blue he called one day. He had failed her, was deeply sorry, and wanted to come home. Over the next few months God did a marvelous work in bringing them back together—a promise fulfilled!

God's promises come in moments of personal renewal, just as the blossoms in spring. Treasure his promises; they can guard your heart through the difficult days to come if you don't try to fulfill them yourself. His promises will come to pass in *his* time.

Chapter 10

A Way to Live

On that day you will realize that I am in my Father,
and you are in me, and I am in you.
JOHN 14:20

Not every branch blessed with spring makes it to the harvest in autumn. Some don't even make it through the spring.

Even though our present situation may not be challenging, there are still unseen dangers in the vineyard. Life begun is life most fragile. The simplest of things can bring a swift end to fruitfulness, or at least diminish the quality of the fruit.

There are two dangers in spring that can destroy the hope of harvest. The first is an unseasonably late freeze. Once the vines have budded, a hard freeze will destroy the buds and leave the vines fruitless. New leaves will shoot, but there will be no crop.

The second danger comes from rare severe hailstorms. Hail can rip the blossoms to shreds, with the same results as a freeze. Leaves will regrow, grape bunches will not.

If only these dangers were as rare in the Father's vineyard! How often I see people touched in incredible ways by the grace and love of God only to watch them fade away as if it had been some passing fad. I find them back in the same place they were before wondering if that moment had been real. What happened? Though they genuinely may have experienced God's touch, they didn't find a way to respond to him so his life would take root in them.

Being in season in the spring means that the branches deepen their connection to the vine. Growth doesn't happen just because God touches us, but because we respond to that touch by allowing him to grow in us. Jesus showed us how this process of fruitfulness can get sidetracked through the parable of the Sower. The seeds did not mature either because people didn't understand what he was doing in them, or because they didn't let their roots go deeply in the soil.

That's why the farmer works so tirelessly in the spring—to prepare the vines for what's coming. In the spring, the vine has few needs. The rains water it, the soil nourishes it, and the weeds are far too small to provide any real challenge to the vine. The farmer, however, is already looking ahead to summer, when the weeds will be much larger and could choke out the vine's life, and when the intense heat will stress the weakened vine.

One day he'll be plowing down weeds and on another spreading fertilizer. All of this is designed to strengthen the vine against the elements and prepare it to live well in the coming days of increased pressure. The best time to prepare is always before the need arises.

That's true of our spiritual journeys as well. If we just live off the moment in times of ease and don't use the time to deepen our friendship with Jesus, we will be caught unaware when trials and temptations come. But too many cannot look beyond the moment. Everything is going so well just the way it is. Why do I need to seek after him, since he seems to be blessing me anyway? Why do I need to read the Scriptures, since God seems to be speaking to me everywhere I turn? These are the same people who will find themselves lost in a crisis they didn't see coming because their relationship with Jesus wasn't deep enough to sustain them.

Spiritual spring is the time to cultivate our connection to the vine so that we have strength in reserve. It is precisely at times of great blessing, when God is so readily present, that patterns for nourishment can be built in our own lives with the most effectiveness. God is easy to find in our reading, our prayers, and our touch with the body of Christ. There is no better time to discover a way to live in him that will hold up to the uncertainties of the future.

I'm convinced that's why Jesus took time to pray in the Garden. He knew the trial that was coming and was deeply distressed. Because he spent time with the Father before the torments of the religious leaders, the injustice of his case, and the brutality of the cross, he had strength to follow God's purpose.

The disciples had no idea what was coming and couldn't stay awake alongside their friend. Jesus knew that their spirits were willing, but their flesh was too weak. They would be overwhelmed by the unfolding events and scatter trying to protect themselves. How do we counteract doing this very thing? By learning how to live in him in the season where the challenges aren't so great.

When I read through the Gospels I'm amazed by the things Jesus *didn't do,* as much as by those things he did. Yes, I marvel at his healings and the miracles as well as the tender moments he had one-on-one with his followers. But I'm also amazed that he didn't spend any time teaching his followers a systematic theology to teach to others, outlining a code of ethics, or giving a prescribed set of rituals to follow. He didn't teach them how to organize a local congregation, plan for a Sunday service, or plot out a daily quiet time.

Those are all things I learned early on in my faith journey as essentials to being a good Christian. Why were they not so important to Jesus? What was he doing with those early followers if he wasn't teaching them what he wanted them to do? He was teaching them how to live.

He lived in the care of his Father, with an eye and ear out for what his Father was doing. He wanted them to know that same relationship. He didn't come to start a new religion or to promote a new morality. He came to reconnect us to the Father, knowing that relationship would shape us in ways laws or rules never could. He had a way for them to live that would transform their lives and make them fruitful in the world. This was done not with techniques and strategies, but through living in the Father.

Jesus tells the story of his Father's vineyard in the middle of his upper room discourse. He is talking about the nature of the relationship he, the Father, and the Spirit want to have with each of the disciples and with each of us.

Learning to live in him is not as easy as following a set of guidelines or practicing a daily or weekly ritual. Knowing him goes on at a heart level that defies all attempts to standardize it. And it isn't so much that we have to build a relationship with him as it is for us to respond to the way he's building one with us. So instead of working through a list of disciplines, it might be better just to open our hearts to him and ask him to show us how he wants to relate to us.

I have three grandchildren and if I want a relationship with them, especially at the younger ages, I'm going to go into their world. If that's true of me relating to a smaller human being, how much more so for the transcendent God to make himself known to one of his creation. I can't build a relationship with him; I can only respond as he guides me.

This process differs for each person. I don't have three steps to give you to make it happen. It begins by letting him show me how much he loves me and then I begin to recognize his fingerprints in my life. Eventually you'll find your way into an ongoing conversation with God about your life and the people in it. This is a process that takes time.

Most of us live as if God doesn't love us until we jump through enough hoops to merit his blessing. We try in our own strength to earn his approval by doing the things we have been taught he expects of us. But you will find the harder you try the more you'll lose sight of him and in the end you'll end up more proud of your accomplishments than you are aware of him.

I encourage you to wake up every morning and ask God to make himself known to you. I pray that prayer often. Then I go through my day looking for ways God impresses his heart on mine—the things he wants to show me and the ways he wants me to treat others. I find myself increasingly ruminating on what God might think of what I'm involved in and what his heart might be in the decisions I face. This is the conversation. It's an ongoing meditation that becomes clearer over time.

It helps to focus our attention on him throughout our day, whether we're driving somewhere or pausing between appointments at work. I keep questions and doubts before him and reflect on them, looking for the tidbits of wisdom or inkling of insight he gives me. How does God engage that conversation? He makes his thoughts known as I'm looking for them. That happens as I go for a walk to pray and listen to him, read the Scriptures, or engage in conversations with others.

As that conversation grows I become more aware of him, more sensitive to the impressions he puts on my mind, and more loving to the people around me. This is the renewing of our mind that gives us a way to live in him that will transcend spring. It will untwist the thought patterns that have distorted our lives with feelings of self-loathing or self-exaltation. We will lose confidence in our efforts and agendas and become more at rest in his unfolding revelation. We'll find ourselves living differently than we used to—less manipulative of people and more caring.

This is the essence of what it means to abide, or dwell in him. It is to engage him and his wisdom in ever-increasing ways in our lives. It is not a matter of learning a set of principles. Don't rush it. Growing into this kind of conversation takes time and happens far more at a heart level than in our minds. It doesn't happen by changing our actions to conform to God's desires, but by getting to know him so well that we think differently. As we think differently, we will live differently.

Even if you've been a believer for a long time and missed out on this conversation, don't waste time being embarrassed about it. Many others have as well. But there's no time like now to start fresh and ask him to show you how he wants to make himself known to you. Without it you will never make it through summer and to the fruitful harvest God has for you.

Those who don't deepen that relationship in spring will find that crisis and stress will create such doubt about God's intentions for you that you'll whither in the stress. I know that was true for me. I lived through so many spring seasons only to find myself unable to sustain my trust in God in the heat of conflict. I would doubt him and myself and would end up frustrated that this spiritual life didn't seem to work as advertised.

And what did God do? He did what no earthly farmer can do. He drew me back into spring again to renew my heart in his presence in hopes that I would find a relationship with him that would sustain me in times of trouble. Real fruitfulness is a long-term process where our growing trust in him works over years to help us learn to follow him.

Nowhere is this more powerfully illustrated than in the vine.

Growing to know him not only influences the next harvest but the one beyond it. Grapes are a two-year crop. The bunches forming now were developed a year before while another crop was coming to fruitfulness. Then the grapes were microscopic in size and hidden in the buds of next year's crop. How the vine was cared for last year will determine the quality of the next crop.

Though Paul talked about the process of sowing and reaping as an important element in our spiritual life, many believers mistakenly think that their spiritual life will flourish without their participation. They assume that grace will cover for their spiritual lethargy, but it will not. Whenever we get just enough of God to survive the day, we've let the process break down and we won't have enough fullness to carry us to fruitfulness. While spiritual growth is God's work in us, it doesn't happen without our intentional participation to abide in him. That's what this book is about.

Spring is where these patterns are set. The roots are encouraged to go deep. The leaves spread their sails to catch the life-giving rays of the sun. The weeds are cut out while they are small; the insects are destroyed before they proliferate. This is the time to give attention to your spiritual way of life. Don't wait for disaster to send you seeking for what is easy to find now.

He wants you to become so confident in his love that when the blossoms fade and the heat begins to rise, we will endure with him as those fragile nubs at the end of our branches become the glorious bunches of grapes the farmer desires.

Chapter 11

A Life-Long Friendship

And so we know and rely on the love God has for us.
1 JOHN 14:16

I used to live on the edge of town, where I could walk out my door and into the cotton fields and plum orchards that stretched for miles behind my home. I didn't own them, but borrowed them each morning as a prayer closet. As I'd walk among the rows, Buffy, my lab and shepherd mix dog, would go with me as she dashed through the fields hoping for a rabbit to chase or a pheasant to flush.

Buffy had walked these fields with me ever since she was a puppy and evidently assumed that they all belonged to me. She would chase after anything that came near, from Dobermans to horses. She even chased off a wild coyote that tried to stare her down. Her protection against the dangers of other animals and the distant roadways rested in her ability to respond to one simple command: Stay!

Buffy knew it well enough, but I'll have to admit that whether or not she obeyed it depended on how close she was to me when I called her. If she was too far away and the temptation too great, she was off, and no amount of yelling would bring her back until the chase was spent. Then she returned with great remorse in her eyes. Even a dog knows it is easier to ask for forgiveness than permission!

Fortunately she always returned at some point and I always kept her close whenever we were near other people or a road.

I love the one thing Jesus asked of his followers when he told them the parable of the vineyard. "Remain," he repeats throughout his lesson . . . ten times to be exact. His command should not be difficult to understand. It's the same as commanding a dog to stay or giving instructions to your child as you plunge together into the midday crowd at the local mall.

When Jesus invites us to remain, however, it is not a request for the moment, but the way he wants us to live. His word spoke of a persistent remaining, as in taking up residence. He doesn't want us to only run to him when trouble strikes or when we need something. He wants us to remain with him all day, every day.

Unlike a wild animal that will only drink when it is thirsty, the branch drinks from the vine continually. It never goes out on its own and never has to come back. It is there all the time. We cannot compartmentalize our spiritual life, making time for God like we do our work or play. Life in Christ permeates everything we do—our work and our play.

Though it sounds fine when we speak of vines, it is a bit jarring when we refer to people. We naturally think of remaining *with* someone, not *in* them. But the level of intimacy that a branch has with the vine is the standard by which Jesus measures our relationship with him. This is an intimate link. Our identity and existence are bound up in the vine.

The early church understood the depth of intimacy that Jesus invited them to discover. They didn't consider themselves born-again Christians, as if they had joined a new club. They lived *in Christ,* daily drawing his life and reflecting his glory. The place it offers us is the same one Jesus shared with his Father. *You will remain in my love, just as I . . . remain in his love.*

What a contrast to everything this world teaches us! If we want anything in this life we have to earn it, vesting our energies to somehow gain the thing we desire. This is not true in God's vineyard.

We don't have to achieve anything. In the springtime of our lives, he makes all things new. He establishes us in himself through Christ, opening our hearts to be sensitive to his presence and his voice.

All we need to do is embrace that friendship. What we tend to do, however, unlike the branches in my father's vineyard, is to continually run off after every distraction or temptation. The most important lesson you'll ever learn in his vineyard is how to remain where he established you. Do that and fulfillment and fruitfulness will grow in your heart no matter what life hurls at you. Fail to do that and you will inevitably end up empty and frustrated.

Scriptures encourage us to cultivate moments throughout our day where we pause, if sometimes only for a few moments, to heighten our awareness of Jesus' presence with us. There we focus our attention on him and his affection for us, freely expressing ours in return. There he soothes our demanding fears, exposes our seductive flesh, or gives insights into the midst of our day. Sometimes his touch comes almost before we even turn our attention toward him; at others it comes after we have lingered, waiting on him and bringing our hearts to rest in his presence.

He is faithful to those moments and by them transforms us ever more into his image, producing in us the fruit we so desire to offer him. And when we remain in that friendship, year after year, through good and difficult times, his fruit continues to grow in us.

The invitation of the vine is not to a short-term friendship. As Jesus looked across those young men in the Garden, he didn't want to use them up in a flash of brilliance. He invited them to a lifelong friendship. His work in them would encompass the whole of their lives. The best fruit comes from the great depths that the passage of time affords.

Unfortunately our society knows so little of the beauty of long-term friendships. We are a transient culture, moving so frequently that lifelong friendships are indeed rare. This is especially true when Christians exploit one another to fill their own needs. Gossip, betrayal, and broken relationships unfortunately are all too common.

Even the advertising of our world preys on our penchant to become quickly bored with anything that becomes too familiar and lures us with the excitement of something new or different.

My wife and I have developed a friendship through more than three years of courtship and now thirty-six years of marriage. Sara and I have had that much practice loving each other and we are finally getting pretty good at it. We've let God shape us alongside each other so that we complement each other far more now than when we first married. We are now reaping the glorious benefits of long-term friendship: private jokes no one else can understand, thinking the same thing at almost the same moment, saying more to each other with a glance and a wink across a crowded room than less-practiced couples can say in a night of conversation. We laugh harder than we've ever laughed and hold each other more tenderly through difficult moments than we ever could have years ago.

Jesus wants the same for us. Every year is meant to be better than the one before because he's grown more familiar to us. Having tasted of his faithfulness over the course of the years we find it more real than we ever dreamed.

Some of the branches in my father's vineyard are more than forty years old, and yet they keep on yielding one harvest after another. Vineyards are long-term crops with more mature vines producing season after season far better than young ones.

As Jesus told the tale of the vineyard he was preparing his followers for the traumatic days they were about to face, days that could make them question everything Jesus had ever said to them. He didn't want their pain and confusion to destroy their friendship. "In this world you will have trouble. But take heart! I have overcome the world."

Will our security in God's love win over misunderstood suffering, unanswered prayers, months of unemployment, or the abuse of friends? This is the essence of fire-tested faith. It endures even the events we cannot understand . . . and it finds its resolve in knowing that God is wholly good and that he can be trusted with our lives. It is only out of this trust that we can discover the mystery of God's grace and wisdom will always be enough to help us overcome any situation.

At the end of his life, alone in a prison cell in Rome, realizing that the churches in Asia were quickly deserting the true gospel for cheap imitations, Paul declared with absolute certainty, "I have kept the faith." Amidst the struggles and fears, the confusions and doubts, don't let go of faith no matter what. Remain in his love, and all he wants to do in you and through you will be done.

"Remain in my love." How much more simply could Jesus have said it? No matter what the challenge, no matter how right our perspective may appear, invest your trust in him today, and every day for the rest of your life. Then you'll know the depth of lifelong friendship.

Chapter 12

Of Fading Blossoms and Future Fruit

Forgetting what is behind and straining toward what is ahead,
I press on toward the goal to win the prize for which
God has called me heavenward in Christ Jesus.

PHILIPPIANS 3:13-14

Spring can't last forever. The pristine beauty of the new shoots and blossoms slowly fade as the lengthening days and increased heat take their toll on the vineyard. Every year since the first dawn, spring has passed into summertime. The young, green leaves weather and darken, their edges fray and split as they face the elements. The blossom petals, small and pale, have long since turned a dusty brown and lie unnoticed on the vineyard floor.

I've never heard a farmer complain of the diminished beauty of his vineyard. He is focused on the harvest, and summer is the next step to getting there. So even though the field looks a bit ragged, he is not concerned. He realizes that this is just part of the process to bring the blossoms to their fruitful splendor.

Unfortunately we're not always so blessed by the process. Unlike the vines in my Father's vineyard, we easily fall in love with the joys of springtime and consider the changing season to be a sign of God's disfavor. I've seen it happen way too often. People who have enjoyed the freshness of spring grow concerned when glory fades, as if they have done something wrong and God is now punishing them.

Instead of letting go of the fading blossoms, they try to hide in past glories. Failing to embrace a greater process, they are only concerned about their temporal comfort and how they look to others. As the season begins to change they resist changing with it. That makes as little sense as the branches of a vine trying to glue the wilted blossoms back on their canes hoping no one will notice.

We seem to forget that while fruit begins in spring, it will never ripen there. In our own spiritual lives we cannot afford the luxury of trying to preserve the past, no matter how much we might have been blessed by it. God moves on, just like the seasons of the vineyard. If we don't move with him we will not be fruitful.

You can almost take a course on church history by visiting in the right order various congregations in your own hometown. In appropriate garb and liturgy you can taste of church life in the Middle Ages, in the Reformation, in the Anabaptist movements, even in the Great Awakening. And you can find churches whose heyday was in the forties and fifties still clinging to the songs and dress of those days.

Many represent a moment of God's renewal frozen in time. Often justifying it as an appreciation of God's work through history, it is usually an attempt to try to hold on to spiritual spring instead of risking the process of change. Why? Were those days any more holy than what God wants to do today? No! They are just more comfortable. But that is also their trap. Staying where we're comfortable doesn't always lead us to the changes God has for our lives.

I have found that the greatest enemy to the process of fruitfulness in our lives is to hold on to something wonderful God did earlier and try to replicate it today. Nothing will detract us from fruitfulness more than building a home where God only wanted us to pitch a tent. This is a journey and you can't reach its end by staying in the same place.

Please understand I have nothing against celebrating the great heritage of faith others carved who went before us. There's much we learn from God's hand moving in the past. And neither do

I champion the notion that God is always in the latest innovation. However, whenever we preserve our traditions at the expense of following God's leading, those traditions and our lives are emptied of power.

I know of nothing more tragic than empty, religious activity where people go through the motions but find no joy or power in them. This can happen when we try to force God's work into our own molds; Jesus warned us against doing so:

> *No one pours new wine into old wineskins. If he does, the new wine will burst the skins, the wine will run out and the wineskins will be ruined. No, new wine must be poured into new wineskins. And no one after drinking old wine wants the new, for he says, "The old is better."*
>
> — LUKE 5:37–39

The Pharisees were once again trying to trap Jesus by accusing his followers of not fasting. Jesus deals with their immediate question by saying that fasting isn't appropriate in times of joy—as he, bridegroom, was with them. But the day was coming when they would fast.

Then he told them that old wineskins, just like our traditions, grow hard and rigid over time. When the wine in them begins to ferment, they are not flexible enough to handle the pressure it puts on the wineskin. Instead of holding the wine, they burst. The wine spills out and the wineskin is destroyed.

It was such a simple picture, yet everyone knew what he was talking about. Anyone who put new wine in an old wineskin lost both. His application, however, was new. Unless the Pharisees and the teachers of the law could find a new wineskin, they could not contain this new work of the Spirit. Their old, rigid understanding of spirituality could not withstand the new wine God's Spirit poured out in the gospel. To be part of God's continuing work in the world they had to change, and their rigid commitment to their own illusion of security would not allow them to do that.

Whenever we hold on to the past instead of following him, our lives will not be fruitful or fulfilled. At every moment we must risk the past to embrace a greater process that will lead us to real fulfillment in him, and in turn, a greater fruitfulness.

Go ahead and risk the joys of spring for a far greater reward. Release the blossoms as they begin to fade, for the coming fruit will be a joy to you and an even greater delight to the Master. The summer will come anyway. There is no use resisting it. You can pretend it is spring all you want, but that will not change reality. It is far better to embrace the summer with God, than to try to hold God to a past where he no longer dwells.

Even if you like the spring, don't fear leaving it. It will come around again. But understand that springtime is not the ideal of a life of faith. It is a wonderful time, indeed, but so is each season of God's working. Our greatest joy is in *enjoying* him regardless of our circumstances.

When the comfort of easier days gives way to greater challenges, you don't have to waste time thinking you have done something wrong or that God has abandoned you. You can remain confident that a new season is at hand. Though it may be less exciting and fraught with more challenges, it is the season where promises become reality.

Embracing the summer season doesn't mean there is something wrong with spring, only that it is over. Tiny rock-hard nubs have replaced the blossoms, but in time those will become the juicy, sweetened grapes that the Father is looking for.

His friendship with us doesn't diminish in the summer; it matures. If we don't seek to preserve the past we can delight in it even as God leads us on in the ongoing process of fruitfulness. You can find him where you are today. You don't have to drag him or yourself back to a past that wasn't half as good as you remember it anyway.

Your best days are not behind you, at least in this vineyard. Each season has its own opportunities. Summer is for those who want to learn what it really means to be fruitful.

Summer

The Fruit Matures

*See! The winter is past; the rains are over and gone
And we rejoice in the hope of the glory of God. Not only so, but
we also rejoice in our sufferings, because we know that suffering
produces perseverance; character; and character, hope. And hope
does not disappoint us, because God has poured out his love into
our hearts by the Holy Spirit, whom he has given us.*

ROMANS 5:2–5

The leaves have grown and the grapes have set. All that is needed for the vine's fruitful harvest is in place. Now it needs to mature in the heat of summer.

Chapter 13

The Long, Hot Days of Summer

Endure hardship as discipline . . .
No discipline seems pleasant at the time, but painful.
Later on, however, it produces a harvest of righteousness
and peace for those who have been trained by it.
HEBREWS 12:11

Unlike the other seasons, summer creeps up slowly. Spring begins with the first dripping of sap from the ends of the freshly pruned canes, autumn with the freshly ripened fruit hanging from the vine, and winter by the first dusting of frost. For farmers, these signs are more accurate than dates scientists mark on calendars.

By the time June 21 arrives in the San Joaquin Valley of Central California, it seems like summer is already half over. Nearly two-dozen days have already passed with temperatures higher than 100 degrees, some pushing 110. Growth isn't as obvious now. Spring was far more spectacular as the landscape of the vineyard seemed to change daily. Fresh growth stretched its way to the heavens until their own weight caused them to curl earthward again.

In summer the growth shifts from the branches and leaves to what is beneath them: the grapes. They are smaller than a BB and almost as hard. But that is about to change.

The branches and leaves continue to grow during this season but not so prolifically. The longer days and abundance of leaves allows sunlight to be converted to more energy than the vine needs.

The excess goes into the grapes. They begin to grow more rapidly, softening as they are pumped full of the sugar produced in the leaves.

Throughout the summer the labor of the farmer settles into the routines of irrigation and cultivation. There's not much he can do now to increase the crop, but his neglect of those duties can bring it to a swift end or severely damage its quality. These are days of hard work, far less beautiful than the blooming vines of spring and far less glorious than the joys of harvest. These are the days of perseverance.

How do we know when summer comes in our own spiritual growth?

It's when the euphoria of spring fades in the struggle of life. No longer does God's work come so easily, no longer does each day seem fresh. It can be brought on suddenly by a crisis in our lives, or more slowly as some internal struggle raises its head. Suddenly we're not as certain of God's love for us, or of our ability to follow him.

If you thought you were responsible for the joys of spring, you'll blame yourself for the onset of summer. Because his presence doesn't feel as immediate, you will wonder if you've offended God in some way, causing him to withdraw from you. Or even worse you'll fear he has removed his blessing and you'll have to work to recover it again.

We weren't meant to always live in spring. Spring is a season where God hovers over us with his bounty and invites us to live more deeply in him and in his joy. But he knows we'll never mature there. Eventually we have to face real life again—the chaos from a world that is no longer in synch with its Creator, and the brokenness where self-centeredness has twisted us.

It's not that God has withdrawn his blessings; it's that he's decided to bless us at a far deeper level. By allowing us to face the reality of life in this age, he is drawing us to the end of ourselves and more deeply into himself. There we will learn to rely on him and his love in ways that will untwist the damage of sin and allow us to be all that he originally created us to be. In the end, that's what makes us truly fulfilled and, in turn, fruitful.

The very things God intends to mature us can also be used to destroy us. The same life-giving sun that beckons the grapes to ripen also creates a hostile climate, which the vines must overcome. Too many days of high temperatures can put stress on the vine that will reduce the size and sweetness of its grapes. The sun also dries out the land, robbing it of the moisture the vine needs to survive. The lengthened days and warmed temperatures allow the insects to multiply rapidly, an ever-present threat to the vines. The weeds, too, benefit from the sun as they continue to mount their assault on the vine's nutrient supply.

Summer has both risks and rewards. It is during the time between spring and harvest that so many believers lose hold of their hope in God and see the glory of his promise fade in the hostile climate around them. Because the fulfillment of the promise is not yet in hand, they give up, thinking that a promise delayed is a promise denied.

The farmer doesn't see summer as a delay; rather, he sees summer as the next step in the process of bringing the promise of spring to the abundance of harvest. His eye is firmly fixed on the formation of that fruit. Summer is not the end. It will not last forever. It will last long enough for the fruit to ripen. Even though it is difficult, it can't be skipped. So he perseveres, not with resigned despair, but with hopeful anticipation.

Ever vigilant, the farmer cares for the vine through the summer, for danger abounds at every turn. He waters the vine when the soil dries up, tears out the weeds wherever they emerge, and destroys the pests that war against the vine.

Our spiritual summers demand the same vigilance of us. We must meet the challenges of summer head-on, persevering so that the harvest is assured. Our flesh will resist, complaining at what we will perceive as God's inactivity. But this is the enemy talking, wanting us to give up, discarding God's promise in anger because it is not yet in our hands. He can even convince us that it is all God's fault. He makes you wonder whether God tricked us with a promise he didn't want to fulfill, or whether he is faithful through difficult days.

The men and women of God who are lauded in the Scriptures are those whose faith has traversed this chasm between promise and harvest. They have endured the onslaughts of summer, drinking deeply of God's goodness and staying the course while the fruit ripens. If we're going to be fruitful in God's kingdom we can do no less.

Chapter 14

The Upside of Trouble

In this world you will have trouble.
But take heart! I have overcome the world.
JOHN 16:33

Have you ever had your faith so challenged you found yourself wondering about God's intentions toward you? *How could God let this happen to me?*

Have you been caught in circumstances that drove you beyond anything you were prepared for, overwhelming you with feelings of inadequacy? *I just don't know what to do.*

Have you lost sight of Jesus when you needed him most? *I can't seem to find him no matter what I do.*

Or, have you felt all alone in a crisis, finding your human relationships weren't strong enough to help you through your pain. *I just couldn't tell anyone, I'd be too embarrassed.*

Welcome to summer.

When it feels as if the tide of your life has swallowed up your growing relationship with Jesus, you can be confident that summer has arrived, whether it slowly snuck up on you or came in the sudden wake of a full-blown crisis. Summertime is the season of struggle. The sun has grown hotter, the fields dustier, and water comes with far less frequency, but it is precisely in those challenges that grapes grow and ripen. Good fruit is born of adversity, that's why we do not need to fear when we encounter difficulties in our lives.

While it might have been so easy a few months earlier to find comfort in God's presence, or to sense his voice, it now seems impossible. Take heart. The cries of summer often make people think they are going backward, but it is precisely in working through these struggles and doubts that your relationship with him deepens. Through summer, you become free of your ambitions, and God is able to transform you ever more into his image.

Without extensive irrigation systems in Israel around the time of Jesus, farmers were forced to depend on recurring rainstorms to water their crops. For plants to survive they had to have roots deep enough in the soil to search out moisture in order to survive under the blazing sun until another storm arrived. Fortunately summer rains are more common there than in Central California where it usually never rains between late April and late October. The vines only survive in that valley because they are irrigated from the run-off of the Sierra Nevada mountains and the large aquifer under the ground.

But even with irrigation, vines are watered to drive the roots deep. My father did it every three or four weeks, depending on the severity of the heat. And when he irrigated, he didn't put a sprinkling of water on the surface, but deep-watered by flooding his field. That forced the roots to go deep instead of loitering near the surface. Deep roots also help anchor the vine and give its roots greater breadth for drawing needed nutrients from the soil.

Of course in Jesus' analogy he is the vine and we are the branches. Branches don't have roots, only the vine does, and certainly Jesus' roots are deep enough to weather any crisis. But the point is still made in the branch's attachment to the vine. If we remain in him, we too will weather the heat of summer. Instead of being defeated by our troubles, we will find that by enduring through them, incredible fruit has been shaped in our lives.

The most compassionate people I know have endured great pain and struggles and know well what others are going through. The most generous people I know have also known scarcity in their own life and want to help others who find themselves there as well. The upside of trouble is that it can bring us to the end of ourselves and open a wide vista into the Father's heart for us and others.

It's not the actual trouble or the struggle that changes us—what changes us is enduring through them with Jesus. Many people spiral into self-pity at the first sign of trouble, either blaming God for not being fair to them or mistakenly thinking God is punishing them for some reason. Live there and you'll grow increasingly bitter and cynical over time. The fruit that will grow will not be his fruit.

For the branch, being in season through the challenges of summer means that we learn to remain in him even beyond our comfort or our understanding. In his parable of the sower, Jesus pointed out that some seeds fell on the rocks where there wasn't much soil. The seeds grew quickly as long as the rains were present, but when the sun stayed out for any length of time, the plant withered and died.

Plants that give little attention to their roots grow quickly and often more impressively than those around them, but it is only external growth. Summer will test the quality of that growth. Jesus interpreted the parable: *Since he has no root, he lasts only a short time. When trouble or persecution comes because of the word, he quickly falls away.*

This is why it is so important for our relationship to deepen with Jesus in the relative ease of spring. Scripture exhorts us to seek God while he is near and easy to find. If we do not learn how to deeply nourish our lives in him when it is easy, there will be no strength to endure the heat of summer. Those who busy themselves with Christian activities at the expense of learning to live in him will do fine when circumstances are easy. Eventually, however, when the rains of spring give way to summer's heat, we will dry up and die.

With plants, the roots grow deeper quite naturally. As the sun dries out the soil from the top down, the roots are drawn downward to where moisture still remains. In our lives it isn't so natural. We often get used to the ease of engaging Jesus when all is well. During some seasons he seems to be everywhere we look. We read the Scriptures and gain new insights, hear teachings that encourage our journey, or find ourselves in conversations that shine his light into our lives.

When trouble comes, however, our hearts are often distracted and it isn't so easy to see him. Many keep doing the same things, hoping the freshness will reappear. Others might give up discouraged that their walk with him has become so difficult. But God has not gone anywhere. Circumstances may be drying up the surface water, but his life is still there for us to embrace. He wants to make himself known in ways other than what we have become accustomed to. All we need to do is see these times as God inviting us deeper—past the goose bumps and the heart flutters—to the treasure of his presence.

Now is the time to turn our hearts more intentionally to him and watch even more for his fingerprints in our lives and listen to his voice in our ears. He is not making himself more difficult to find; it is our circumstances that do that. Now we have the opportunity to draw more deeply into him. So if reading the Bible has become difficult and lifeless, keep reading, looking more intently to see what he is making clear to you. When your fellowship with others grows stale, don't give up and withdraw into yourself. Stay in those relationships as God shapes them to take you deeper.

God doesn't use the stress of summer to teach us how to live without him. He uses it to invite us to find him at a deeper level beyond our own ease and convenience. Our life in him is not dependent on the ease of our circumstances but by the wonder of his person. He wants us to know him so well that we do not falter in times of pressure. Though Jeremiah was not talking about a grapevine in his vision, his words are just as true for the branch that learns to draw continually from the vine: *It does not fear when heat comes; its leaves are always green. It has no worries in a year of drought and never fails to bear fruit.* (Jeremiah 17:8)

That's the heritage of deep-watered roots: We never lack, no matter how desperate the situation. We all will periodically face seasons of struggle and times of need. Don't think of them as an indication that your spiritual life has suddenly taken a downturn. They are part of growing; you can prepare for them by learning how to stay connected to Jesus and draw from the depths of his roots into the Father. That will enable us to withstand any trouble or disappointment, any onslaught of doubt or fear.

Enduring and persevering in relationship with Jesus is precisely the environment that fruit flourishes in. Every major voice in the New Testament underscores the reality of our faith flourishing in a hostile climate.

> *Consider it pure joy, my brothers, whenever you face trials of many kinds, because you know that the testing of your faith develops perseverance. Perseverance must finish its work so that you may be mature and complete, not lacking anything.*
>
> — JAMES 1:2–4

The optimum growing temperature for the vineyard is in the 80s and low 90s. Above that, the heat takes its toll on the vine. It's a mixed blessing, since the number of sunlight days we have over the summer make this a prime place to raise grapes. Our arid climate rarely offers us a cloudy day throughout the summer. Nonetheless, if the heat becomes too excessive, it will sap the branches of their strength and diminish the quality of the fruit.

Don't forget, Jesus' teaching on the vineyard accompanied the most severe trial his young followers had ever faced. In the next few hours Jesus would be betrayed and crucified. He warned them he was leaving them and fear ran rampant in the room. Again and again he appealed to them, "Do not let your heart be troubled." He didn't hide the fact that his disciples must endure pain in this world. But they need not despair; he had overcome the world.

James picks up that same message: *Consider it pure joy, my brothers, whenever you face trials of many kinds.* It is a cause for rejoicing because the perseverance produced in adversity is what brings the promise to completion. Those early followers wanted us to know that we don't have to despise painful circumstances or seek for God to change them, but instead see his hand in them accomplishing something far grander in our lives.

In these passages the writers never seem to indicate that God was the cause of their trials. He does not need to measure our faith, as if he does not know its depths. He does not orchestrate our crises any more than we would for our own children. Life in a fallen age provides plenty of opportunities for trouble and challenge.

When trials come we have two choices. We can either respond in faith, allowing suffering to become part of the maturing process, or we can respond with anger or resignation and waste the opportunity. God can take the most despicable of circumstance and weave it into the maturing process. He promised us that we would never meet a test greater than we could endure, and that he would always provide a way for grace to triumph over evil.

That's all perseverance means: to persist in the face of difficulty. Keep coming to God in spite of your hurts, doubts, or anger. He can handle it. "Remain in me" is the motto of the vineyard, and at no time is that counsel more important than during the stresses of summer.

The most transforming moments of my life have come in the midst of pain, where I can no longer rely on my own power and wisdom and instead come to new places of rest in the Father's love. He has held me through economic loss, the betrayal of close friends, the deceit of colleagues, and the uncertainty of injury or disease.

Am I grateful for such experiences? No, I can't quite say that either. But I can say that God does some of his greatest work in the depths of incredible pain. I'm still enjoying the benefits of his work long after the wounds have healed.

When I see God so dramatically change my life in the midst of such ugly circumstances I never have to fear anything that might come. His love is able to hold us in the darkest places.

Chapter 15

The Faithful Provider

He who did not spare his own Son,
but gave him up for us all—
how will he not also, along with him,
graciously give us all things?

ROMANS 8:32

The Israelites began as a nomadic people. Growing vineyards was unthinkable. Unlike wheat, vines aren't planted in the spring and harvested a few months later. It takes five years to bring a newly planted vineyard into full production. When God promised his people vineyards he was telling them he would settle them down in safety long enough to partake of their fruit. His work in them was not just for the moment. When Jesus told the parable of the vineyard to his closest friends, it would have carried a meaning far more significant to them because of the unique place vineyards played in the history of Israel as special symbols of God's provision and care.

Israel's vineyards became the symbol of God's promise to allow them to settle in one place for an extended period of time so they could enjoy the fruit of a vineyard. When they settled in Canaan they became the beneficiary of vineyards they didn't plant—a sign of God's abundance. When they returned from the exile in Babylon, God reassured them that they would once again be planted in Canaan and have the chance to plant vineyards.

When God blessed his people you could see it in their vineyards. He promised them weather tailor-made for their crops if they would keep him first in their hearts. But when they turned from him they would lose their vineyards either to an occupying army or from lack of water.

There are not many things so desperate-looking as a withered vineyard. When vines die it is not like a corn crop falling victim to a drought. No matter how great the damage to the corn, it is still only one year's loss. Next year's corn can be replanted and a full crop harvested. Not so with the vine. If it is destroyed, crops are wiped out for years to come.

In these times of want, God would beckon them back to his side promising them that they would be planted once again and take root in their land. The vineyards would once again be planted and they would feast on its fruit.

So it goes through much of the Old Testament. Firmly set in the minds of the disciples as they gathered around Jesus in that vineyard on their last night together was the significance of the grapevine as a symbol of God's provision. The Lord's blessing and discipline were measured in Israel's vineyards and so was his withholding of that provision when their hearts wandered after false gods. Seemingly God used the connection between Israel's spirituality and their comfort as a demonstration of spiritual realities. When they sought God, he gave life. When they turned away from him, they experienced death.

Jesus, however, showed his followers a Father that did not want to make them conform to his ways by alternating between punishment and reward but through winning them with his love. He was their Father too, who would be with them through everything. While his message in the Old Testament seemed to be "Follow me and avoid trouble," Jesus made it clear that living in this world would bring adversity, but that God's love could work in the midst of trouble and then overcome them.

Failure to understand how God's work in us changed when Jesus came will lead people to see every moment of need or disease as proof that God either doesn't care about them or is powerless to help them. They see their pain as his punishment and instead of being drawn to his love at such moments, they either push him away thinking he is its cause, or they expend all their energy trying to get God to take it away.

You don't have to walk with God long to know that even though he could do so, he does not override every adverse or painful situation in our lives. And the fact that he doesn't is not proof that he doesn't love us. The joy of the early believers was found in knowing that God was not the cause of their troubles but the one who wanted to accomplish a higher purpose through them.

Paul and Barnabas encouraged the early churches with these words, "We must go through many hardships to enter the kingdom of God." Encouragement? I'm sure most people would consider that bad news unless, of course, they were already suffering. Paul and Barnabas wanted to show that their hardships were not a sign of God's disfavor, but something that would help people see the kingdom more clearly.

That doesn't mean those who suffer have a greater participation in the kingdom, but rather that as our fleshy ambitions are confronted and overcome in moments of extremity we will be increasingly free to participate in God's reality.

God is not the author of our pain; he was in it to give us life. Throughout Jesus' story of the vineyard his Father constantly hovers in the background. He is not just the gardener who prunes, but the loving Father who provides everything his children need to participate in his life.

There is nothing my father wouldn't do to make his vineyard more fruitful and to overcome all the elements that tried to destroy his vines. Though my father did as much as he could for his vines— irrigating and fertilizing to enrich the soil—he was not always able to overcome all the forces of nature. He was at times as much a victim of the elements as each vine in his vineyard.

God, however, can superintend every detail of his vineyard, monitor every circumstance, and overcome any enemy of growth. He is not only the caretaker of the vineyard, but he is also Master over all creation and the force behind every stage of our growth. When you recognize that God often chooses to be our provider in the midst of our difficulties instead of saving us from them, you will be free to embrace his love regardless of the circumstance you are in.

Certainly God is able to change any of our circumstances and even invites our requests for him to do so. But if he chooses not to remove our adversity, we can still be at rest in knowing that adversity can also be an important factor in the process of fruitfulness. It is not the most enjoyable part, but it is almost always the most effective part. The Father of all knows which hardships to fight against on the vine's behalf and which ones are necessary for the vine to be fruitful.

This reality has changed my prayer life. I used to cry out to God, "If you love me, God, how can you let this happen?" I now find myself praying, "I know you love me even in this, please help me see you here and know how to follow you."

If you're having a difficult time trusting the Father in the circumstances you face today, it's only because you don't know him as well as he wants you to. Ask him and he will help you find his love even in the darkest places.

I like Eugene Peterson's observation about the work of Christ in our age. Whenever the New Testament talks about Jesus taking his seat at the right hand of the Father when all has been put under his feet, Peterson translated it as *Jesus will get the last word on everything and every one.*

My father always had the last word in his vineyard. He was the last one to walk the rows after pruning and tying, grape picking and raisin harvesting. He would pick any bunches that had been missed, tie in vines that had come loose from the wires, or pick up raisins that had fallen on the ground.

I love that Jesus getting the last word on everything. No matter what you're going through today—no matter how painful your circumstances or broken your relationships—Jesus will have the final say. He may not have the last word today, but today isn't the end.

Nothing is complete until it is resolved in him. Everything else is just part of the process.

Chapter 16

A Peek at God's Priorities

And we pray this in order that you may live a life
worthy of the Lord and may please him in every way:
bearing fruit in every good work, growing in the knowledge of God.
COLOSSIANS 1:10

There's nothing a farmer likes to do more than peek.

Throughout the growth of his crop, my father was always peeking to gauge the health of the vine and anticipate the bounty of this harvest. Anytime between the first budding and the final day of harvest, I could ask my father, "How does the crop look?" and without hesitation he always had an answer.

"About average." Or, "Looks like 20 percent above normal."

Even when the grape bunches are smaller than the eraser on my pencil, he's already seen them, looked at how many grapes fill those bunches, and how many bunches hang from each vine—that all takes some serious peeking.

So when I think of a grape farmer, the image that comes most quickly to mind is when he reaches into a vine with both hands, pulling back the leaves and peeking into every nook and cranny. He is as delighted by every bunch he sees as a child finding brightly wrapped packages with his name on them under a Christmas tree.

This peeking continues even in the days after the harvest—just in case one of those bunches had been missed by the harvesters. There is nothing more important to a farmer than the fruit growing in his field. After all, why else plant a vineyard?

In Jesus' lesson on the vineyard, he tells us that his Father is no different. Nine times in his brief sermon is reference made to fruit or fruitfulness. (John 15:1-17) Everything the Father does in his vineyard is geared to making each branch on the vine fruitful.

In a process we'll look at in greater detail when we get to winter, if a branch doesn't bear fruit it is cut off. No sense wasting the vine's energy on what will not bear fruit. If a branch does bear fruit the farmer cuts it too—not off, but trims it so that it can be more fruitful. Fruit, fruit, fruit! That is the Father's priority, and unless we come to share it we will always be frustrated with the Lord's dealing in our lives.

Unfortunately, we haven't all come to the kingdom of God with that same priority. Most people have been bribed into this kingdom with God's other promises.

- Some were offered security in the face of their fears. Surely, they think, there is nothing more important to God than making sure my circumstances never again make me feel insecure.

- Others were extended a rescue in a time of great need. Surely, there is nothing more important to God than making sure I am never in need again.

- Others found forgiveness and cleansing from their guilt and shame. Surely, there is nothing more important to God than protecting me from any temptation that will cause me to sin.

- And some found him a source of healing for their ravaged souls. Surely, there is nothing more important to God than making sure I am happy and never hurt again.

Think again! Is God's greatest priority our feelings of security, safety, or happiness? Many people, confident that it is, find themselves in great confusion when those expectations are not satisfied.

In the vineyard, however, Jesus said that God's priority is to make you fruitful. Our priority, however, is often not so noble. We would much rather be happy or at the very least comfortable. Since God's priority will carry the day, as long as we hold to any objective but fruitfulness we'll find ourselves in continual conflict with God's work in us.

For some this talk of fruitfulness may seem a far cry from our early discussion of fulfillment. *That your joy may be full* may seem to have little in common with *that you bear fruit.* But a farmer knows that the two are directly linked. Fruit only results from fullness. And the Father knows that only in our fruitfulness will we find his kind of joy.

Healthy vines produce fruit; stressed vines do not. A vine poorly pruned, poorly nourished, or encountering a severe lack of water will cast off its fruit in order to keep itself alive for future seasons. No vine left to itself will be fruitful; it will instead become a sprawling mass of fruitless leaves and branches. Attacked by insects and weakened by lack of care, there will not be enough life to bear any fruit. Neither would we be able to bear fruit if God granted us every one of our ambitions and every quest for comfort.

That's why the Father trains and disciplines his vines. Though it causes some rough going in the short term, he wants them to know the fullness of joy that comes from being fruitful.

As Jesus approached Jerusalem for the last time, he told his disciples that the hour for his death had come. Then in what appears to be a spontaneous burst of emotion, we see the battle Jesus fought. "Now my heart is troubled, and what shall I say? 'Father, save me from this hour'?" Isn't that the cry that springs most easily to mind when we encounter trouble? It also did for him.

Certainly Jesus wanted to forgo the pain, but he chose something better. *No, it was for this very reason I came to this hour. Father, glorify your name!* (John 12:23–28) Instead of crying out for his own salvation, he put God's glory first. He sought God's glory over his own comfort, and in so doing showed us the way to be fruitful.

The prayer that is most effective for us to pray in summertime is, *Father, be glorified.* When we look for his glory at the risk of our own comfort, we'll be able to participate in God's unfolding purpose in us.

A God preoccupied with our personal convenience would never have allowed persecution to scatter the church in Judea, or Paul to battle a thorn in the flesh, or James to die by Herod's sword. Obviously God is motivated at a level far higher than our personal convenience. Through all of our adversities he seeks a deeper fruitfulness and uses our circumstances for a greater redemption.

As much as God delights in blessing his children, the intent of that blessing is that we might be a blessing to others. The reason God chose Abraham was not just to bless him but also to make him and his seed a blessing to the whole world. The only priority that drives the Master of the vineyard is to bring us to fruitfulness.

That's also why the farmer peeks so often. He is not just estimating the size of the crop, he is also assessing the health of it. Everything a farmer does is linked to this peeking. Growing a crop is a dynamic process, demanding constant adjustment to an ever-changing environment. There is no schedule to follow that will work successfully every year. You have to observe the vine and its needs in light of the current weather and daily events that impact the vineyard.

He watches over the fruit growing in our lives, carefully tending to its development and thereby ensuring the harvest to come. Nothing delights his heart more than finding his vines spilling over with fruit. That's the reason he plants them and nourishes them. Consequently, there is no greater demonstration of worship or honor than letting the Father bear his fruit in us.

Fruitfulness is not optional. It will take us to some dark valleys, but even in our most difficult moments he will be there peeking. Always keeping his eye on us so that he can give us abundance in the midst of our sacrifice, healing for our hurts, courage in the face of fear, and peace that can flourish even in crisis.

Chapter 17
What Do You Mean, Fruitful?

But the fruit of the Spirit is love, joy, peace,
patience, kindness, goodness, faithfulness,
gentleness and self-control.
GALATIANS 5:22–23

Imagine you've arrived at my father's vineyard during the high days of harvest. "Sit here," my father says, "while I get you some of the fruit from my vineyard." Immediately you picture a bulging bunch of vine-ripened grapes, their green color dusted with the faintest touch of gold from the sugar packed inside. You can almost taste the sweet juice exploding in your mouth with each bite.

What if, however, when he returns he brings you a bowl of boiled grape leaves, or a plate of stir-fried vine bark?

You would be shocked! Everyone knows that you don't grow a grapevine for leaves or bark. Though a local ethnic dish is garnished with cooked grape leaves, no one around here has any doubt about the fruit of the grapevine: round succulent grapes. Chew on some leaves if you like, or even the canes. But after you've bitten into the grapes you'll be satisfied by nothing else on the vine.

So what is fruitfulness to the Father? Throughout my life as a believer, I've heard it defined anywhere from winning new converts to church size or book sales. Since few people consider themselves fruitful, they usually think it's the very thing they lack.

If they are effective in leading a Bible study they are sure that real fruitfulness lies in bringing new converts to the kingdom. If they are evangelistically successful, then they think real fruit lies in practically serving people in need. If they are serving people in need, they only do it because they can't do the "real" work of the kingdom, which is teaching great numbers of people.

On and on the cycle goes, few of us ever hearing God say with delight, "Well done!" It seems we're just not quite sure what it is he really wants of us.

Part of our confusion about fruitfulness stems from our desire to quantify everything, including what we consider to be measures of success—for example, number of converts, bodies in a meeting, or the reach of our influence. Add to that an incomplete and skewed view of Scripture's definition of fruitfulness and it's no wonder our view is blurred.

The Old Testament uses the term *fruitfulness* almost exclusively to refer to having babies—progeny. *Fruitful* is used thirteen times in Genesis, and twelve of those times specifically refer to increasing in number, mostly through bearing offspring. From God's first instructions to the animals he created to his promises to the patriarchs, fruitfulness was specifically linked with an increase of people.

Only a few references hint at God's deeper view of what it means for us to be fruitful in his kingdom. Psalm 72:3 links fruit with righteousness and Isaiah 32:17 extends that application: *The fruit of righteousness will be peace; the effect of righteousness will be quietness and confidence forever.* But perhaps the clearest reference comes in Hosea 10:12: *Sow for yourselves righteousness, reap the fruit of unfailing love, and break up your unplowed ground; for it is time to seek the Lord, until he comes and showers righteousness on you.*

Fruit here is seen as an expression of righteousness that comes from the unfailing love of the Father. Scripture's definition of fruitfulness deepens beyond a simplistic increase of numbers and begins to define it as the depth of our character. In the New Testament, that transition continues. Fruitfulness is *exclusively* seen as the demonstration of

God's transforming power in the character of his people.

John the Baptist encourages us to *produce fruit in keeping with repentance.* In Philippians 1:11, Paul exhorts believers to be *filled with the fruit of righteousness that comes through Jesus Christ—to the glory and praise of God.* In Ephesians 5 he contrasts the difference between the fruit of light (goodness, righteousness, and truth) with the fruitlessness of darkness.

Finally, in Galatians 5:22–23, a passage long revered for its profound simplicity and clarity, he lists the fruits that God desires from his people: love, joy, peace, patience, kindness, goodness, faithfulness, gentleness, and self-control.

This is the fruit God wants for you. It has nothing to do with your activity or anything you can count with numbers. Fruitfulness is a transformed life that demonstrates God's character simply by the way we live in the world. When this fruit fills our lives we will find ourselves engaging people in ways that allow the kingdom to go forward in the world.

The first three of these fruits—love, joy, and peace—are often referred to as blessings that God bestows on his children. He gives us the capacity to love, fills our life with his joy, and gives peace that goes beyond anything we can understand. People who live in these realities are infectious. When you live in God's love you will share it freely with others, no longer using them for your own needs. You will exhibit a joy deeper than the rise and fall of your circumstances and will not demand others make you happy, but seek to better their lives. And when you have peace even in the midst of difficult circumstances you will be a rock others can find hope in.

The second set of three—patience, kindness, and goodness—describe how we should treat others. Being patient with all instead of frustrated or demanding, kind instead of self-seeking, and good with an eye toward what is right and just will endear you to others, even those who don't see life the way you do. When these are fruits in your life you won't have to *act* patient, kind, or good—you will *be* patient, kind, and good.

Finally, the last three—faithfulness, gentleness and self-control—mark the demeanor of someone who is being transformed by God's character and again will make you the kind of person others will gravitate toward. You will be faithful through good times and bad, not just when it benefits you. You will be gentle in spirit, especially with those who disagree with you rather than trying to force them into your mold. And when you have yourself under control you will not act at the whim of your own passions or others' attempts to manipulate you.

These are not difficult concepts to understand. They are only difficult to live out daily. What would someone look like who could demonstrate love, joy, peace, patience, kindness, goodness, faithfulness, gentleness, and self-control in each situation he or she encountered? I think he would look just like . . . well—he would look like Jesus.

Fruit is borne in our character. Fruitfulness has nothing to do with how many Bible studies I've taught, how much money I've given, or how many people I've led to Christ, nor has it any attachment to any other religious activity. It is the transformation of our lives so that we reflect God's nature to the culture around us. In John 15 the call to fruitfulness and Jesus' new command for us to love one another like we've been loved are one and the same.

Only by knowing how loved we are by him can we even begin to care about others. During this process of growth and maturity, his love becomes increasingly real in our daily life. The fruits of the Spirit are not what we can make ourselves do for a moment, but what God produces in us for a lifetime. As he takes shape in us it is how we respond to people in the spontaneity of the moment, not how we are supposed to act

If the objective of our growing relationship with Jesus is not for him to transform us into his image with ever-increasing glory, then it means nothing! Who hasn't known people who can do great things for God, or even speak with great wisdom, but whose engagements with people lack love, patience, or gentleness? Their arrogance and anger mar all else they have accomplished. 1 Corinthians 13 is right: Without love we're just a loud crashing sound, negating whatever benefit we think we render to people.

What the world waits to see is a people who demonstrate God's character by the way they treat one another and even by how they treat those who don't see the world like they do. Are we ready to lay down our lives for others the way Jesus did simply because we care so deeply for them? If people don't see that life in us, why else would they believe? Jesus said our loving was all that the world needed to see to know what God is like.

Jesus didn't spend much time teaching his disciples to plan crusades or door-to-door campaigns. He had already told them earlier that evening that the fruit was what both the Father and the world were looking for: *By this all men will know that you are my disciples, if you love one another.* (John 13:35) For all our institutions and technological expertise, we are sorely lacking in our ability to demonstrate to the world a self-sacrificing community where there is love, forgiveness, and honor instead of backstabbing, manipulating, and complaining.

Unless intimate love overflows in his church, we are only a loud noise that the world will never comprehend. Each time we lay down our lives for another person we allow this world to see what happened two/thousand years ago at Calvary.

This is the fruit of the vineyard. The Father's goal is to see his character filling our lives and spilling out like grape bunches on an overloaded vine. When we realize it is his passion, it will be ours as well.

Chapter 18

If You . . .

Let us not become weary in doing good,
for at the proper time we will reap a harvest
if we do not give up.
GALATIANS 6:9

In the vineyards of this world, branches don't have freedom of choice. They are silent victims of whatever the farmer or his workers decide will be their lot.

Each winter as I pruned vines in my father's vineyard, I had total freedom to shape the vine any way I chose. I decided which branches would remain and which would be cut off. I was master of that vine, and I chose at times almost on a whim which branches might be robust enough to promise a good harvest ahead. The branches had nothing to say about it, no volition of their own. They had no ability to prune themselves even if they wanted to, or stick themselves back on the vine after I had cut them off. They were victims, pure and simple, without any voice or choice in the matter.

But here the Father's vineyard takes another major departure from the earthly one. In his vineyard the branches have their own will. No one compels them to grow. They don't have to stay connected to the vine. We are active participants in the process of fruitfulness. It is not automatic or up to God alone.

People often use the expression *unconditional love* to describe

God's love. I've always been uncomfortable with that term, not because God's love has conditions but because there is no such thing as conditional love. Real love is affection for another regardless of their actions. Love endures forever.

But there is no such thing as unconditional growth in the Father's vineyard. He invites us to participate in this magnificent process. Jesus conveyed that truth to his own followers with a simple two-letter word: *If.* Five times in his parable of the vineyard Jesus uses *if.* Each time it is followed by a simple statement highlighting the role that the branch plays in the vineyard:

- *If* a man remains in me and I in him, he will bear much fruit.
- *If* anyone does not remain in me, he is like a branch that is thrown away and withers.
- *If* you remain in me and my words remain in you, ask whatever you wish, and it will be given you.
- *If* you obey my commands, you will remain in my love.
- You are my friends *if* you do what I command.

If. A simple word to state simple realities. Do this and that will happen, don't do it and something else will. Cause and effect. Reaping and sowing. These are simple facts, simply stated, without loopholes or mitigating circumstances. This is the way God has set things up. Choose to come along, or choose not to. The working is all his, the decision is ours.

However, our free will does not mean that the branches have the run of the vineyard. This is the Father's vineyard. He made it and he determined how it would function. We are free to choose whether or not we want to be part of it, but we cannot change the way God's vineyard functions in order to please ourselves. We can't enjoy the benefits without cooperating in the process.

I've met many people who want to mature in their relationship with God. They want his favor and blessing. Who would say no to that? But even with that desire, many of those persist in walking by their own wisdom or desires. Somehow, they hope, grace will extend beyond their own selfishness and failure to submit to God's ways.

While growing up I always wanted the money that Dad paid us for working in the vineyard, but I never wanted to do the work to get it. I faced the same attitude in my children when they were young. They liked being the beneficiaries of the work that needed to be done around the house—clean clothes and dishes—but they struggled with being participants in the process of gaining them.

For a branch in God's vineyard this simply does not work. The *if* clauses of this passage compel us to make the choice of whether or not we will accept his offer of friendship by how we respond to him.

If we cooperate with him, an array of dazzling opportunities is offered to us. If we do not, we are confronted with certain consequences. The branch dries up and is thrown away. Why? Because one powerful reality lies behind all of Jesus' teachings on the vineyard: "Apart from me you can do nothing." When we cut ourselves off from relationship with Jesus, we are incapable of doing anything in God's kingdom. This doesn't mean we can't be busy in any number of religious activities on his behalf, but none of these activities will bear the true fruit of his kingdom.

We can become distracted from Jesus' involvement in our lives and hardly even notice it. His blessing still seems to accompany us even as we get by on our own strength, unaware of the creeping death that has been unleashed. Then one day we wake up feeling empty or stressed by the demands on our lives. We wonder why God doesn't seem as close to us as before, never recognizing that we have pulled away from the source of life.

Simple neglect of our friendship with Jesus is the biggest danger any of us will ever face. And once we no longer draw life from him we will try and draw it from the world around us. Vines are crafty plants, always looking for nourishment wherever they can find it. They are notorious for rooting wherever they are given the chance. All a cane has to do is fall to the ground—the same buds that are meant to produce fruit and leaves will instead produce roots. It happens so simply that it is one of the chief ways vines are propagated on earth, but not in the Father's kingdom!

Once a branch grows its own roots, it no longer needs the vine. But branches are not supposed to have roots—just canes, leaves, and fruit. What a picture of our own lives! Even while we seek to follow Jesus, the enemy lures us with opportunities to sink our roots into the simplest things. Promising instant gratification, the devices of this world offer no true nourishment and no ultimate satisfaction.

That's why the *if* clauses focus on our relationship with him. *If* we remain in him we will bear much fruit. *If* we remain in him we can ask whatever we wish and it will be given to us. *If* we obey his words we'll remain in his love. We are his friends *if* we do what he commands. *If* we don't, we'll wither and die.

Our task is to remain inside the relationship he's established by getting to know him and by learning to follow him. Every benefit of the vineyard flows from this growing friendship. He does not love us less if we don't participate in it, but neither will we benefit from that love. The father in the tale of the prodigal son did not love his son less when he was living in sin or slaving for the hog farmer. It's just that his father's love did him no good when he would not participate in it.

When we wander away from him, disillusioned that God's promises didn't meet our expectations, we need to be honest enough to consider whether we responded to him in a way that allowed his life to grow in us. We'll often find we didn't. All you have to do, like the prodigal son, is return to the Father and you will find open arms waiting to receive you and restart the relationship he most desires.

For too many decades many have thought of a religious life as the creed we confess or the public declarations we can make. Words are cheap. Jesus invites us to actually embrace a friendship with him where we learn to recognize his voice, understand his ways, and follow his desires.

Every bit of fulfillment and fruitfulness in our lives flows from that simple reality.

Chapter 19

What About the Unfruitful Branch?

If anyone does not remain in me, he is like a branch that is thrown away and withers; such branches are picked up, thrown into the fire and burned.

JOHN 15:6

Fruitless branches are obvious. The branch itself may look fine, but the canes that spring from it are withered and sickly. Few if any of them will even reach up to the wire intended to support them.

I saw it happen a thousand times and each time it seems like such a waste. It takes many years for a branch to develop, and each branch holds the potential for bearing much fruit. But when it was obvious that a branch was no longer capable of bearing fruit, I had to cut it off.

I'd fall to my knees beside the vine and pull the pruning saw from my back pocket. Unfolding the blade I would saw off the fruitless branch, tossing the dead wood into the middle of the row.

So it is in God's vineyard. Branches are designed to bear fruit and when they fail to do so there is no other way to use them. They are cut off, gathered up, and burned in the fire. What else can be done with them? They are not like other varieties of wood that can be crafted into furniture or used to build things.

Some people use grape canes for craft projects. They twist the canes together to form a wreath and then decorate it with dried flowers, wooden geese, and billowy ribbons. I've never liked these wreaths. I've lived too long on a grape ranch to think of dead branches as anything other than fire fuel or fertilizer for next year's crop.

The Gardener prunes away those branches that do not bear fruit and tosses them into the fire. "Bear fruit or burn," could be the theme of John 15. I used to see so much of the language of Scripture as a threat to either do God's will or suffer the punishment . . . of course this passage would evoke the ultimate threat of hell and prey on people's worst fears.

But Jesus wasn't threatening his followers that night. He was inviting them into his love. You can't begin a relationship with Jesus based on fear—it will not lead you to fruitfulness. Jesus wanted them to understand that without a fruitful relationship with him their lives wouldn't count for much. He didn't want them to reduce his work to a religion based on human performance. He wanted them to discover the fullness of life in him.

Some of the stories from Jesus' life that have bothered me the most were of the times Jesus turned away seemingly promising candidates for the kingdom. A man wanted to follow him, but he needed to bury his father first. Jesus' response was harsh: *Let the dead bury their own dead, but you go and proclaim the kingdom of God.* (Luke 9:60)

Or what of the time when the rich young ruler wanted to follow Jesus, but Jesus was only going to let him do so if he would sell everything he owned and give it to the poor? The young man left discouraged because he was not willing to do so.

Once Jesus even chased off the crowd of more than five thousand who had eaten the miraculous lunch of multiplied bread and fish, and then pursued Jesus around the Sea of Galilee. To these he said, "Eat my flesh and drink my blood." The crowd didn't understand his cryptic words and went away confused and disillusioned, wondering if he was inviting them to cannibalism. What bothers me is that Jesus didn't stop them. He didn't run after them and straighten out their misunderstanding: "Hey, come back! I was talking about communion."

Why did he eliminate these people with challenges certainly

more difficult than many new converts today would be able to bear? Or was Jesus looking at something deeper? Could he see that these were branches that were not going to root deep enough to bear fruit? The first man would always cater to his family at the expense of the kingdom. The money of the young ruler would always be his real god. The crowd was looking only for free lunch, lacking the faith that would endure the many other times when God's activity would defy their reason.

Perhaps Jesus realized that without some choice for change these people would not be fruitful and would need to be cut off anyway.

People who want only the smallest bite of salvation in order to feel confident that they will escape hell constantly amaze me. The Father has opened to us a glorious kingdom where we can live in him and know the fullest joy. Why settle for less?

God is willing to do anything to help us find our way into a relationship with him. Jesus told another parable to illustrate his Father's heart for the vineyard. Though the vineyard that Jesus used in this parable is full of figs, the application of his teaching is no less vital to our understanding.

> *A man had a fig tree, planted in his vineyard, and he went to look for fruit on it, but did not find any. So he said to the man who took care of the vineyard, "For three years now I've been coming to look for fruit on this fig tree and haven't found any. Cut it down! Why should it use up the soil?"*
>
> *"Sir," the man replied, "leave it alone for one more year, and I'll dig around it and fertilize it. If it bears fruit next year, fine! If not, then cut it down."*
>
> — LUKE 13:6–9

No farmer would expect a vine to be in full production in three years, but it is extremely unusual for a vine to grow that long without any fruit appearing.

He is ready to cut it down and replace it with a new vine that will bear fruit, but the caretaker here has a better hope: "Let's give it another chance; I'll do everything I can to encourage its fruitfulness, and then if it still doesn't bear fruit, we'll cut it down."

Jesus tells the parable to let the caretaker's heart reveal the Father's. Here again he differs from the farmer who only looks at the bottom line. He sees potential where we often miss it and is willing to invest all his resources in one more attempt at fruitfulness. Cutting off the unfruitful is never God's first choice; it is only his last resort.

God still has hope for fruitfulness even if it feels as though you've squandered the preceding years. If you are still hungry and willing to respond to the Father, your time is not up yet.

Only Jesus can make us fruitful as he lives his life through us. Stay plugged into the vine. If you do that, you'll have more fruit than you know what to do with.

Chapter 20

Life Giving Nourishment

Remain in me, and I will remain in you.
No branch can bear fruit by itself;
it must remain in the vine.

JOHN 15:4

Tying vines is potentially the most painful of farm duties. Each cane remaining on a freshly pruned vine must be wrapped around the wire before the sap begins to flow. Often that put us out in the vineyard while frost still clung to the canes. Since we were by how many vines we tied, speed was of the essence.

Every once in a while, however, in my haste I wouldn't get all the canes tightly secured. One of them would slip off the wire, pick up speed as it uncoiled itself, and smack me on my frozen cheek. I don't know if you've ever been slapped in the face on a subfreezing morning, but I can only commend it as an excellent form of torture.

For me, pain was almost always followed by anger, and often before rational thought set in I would rip the offending cane out of the vine for its vile deed. Only then would the destruction I had caused sink home. Not wanting to be caught tying a vine with four canes when they're all supposed to have five, I would shove the base of the cane back into a cranny in the vine and tie it back on the wire. No one would be the wiser.

At least until the sap didn't flow. And though it still might be stuck into the vine, we've already seen that if it is not attached to the vine, nothing will happen. Not one bud will swell, not one leaf will sprout. It is dead.

Someone walking through the vineyard can't even see the most significant contribution the vine makes to the branch. It goes on deep beneath the scraggly bark. Through small capillary tubes, nutrients and water flow up through the roots, travel through the trunk, and spread out through every branch until they reach every leaf and maturing grape bunch. This life-giving sap makes the difference between a branch that is fruitful and one that is fit only for destruction.

The only time you get to see this flow of sap is early in the spring, before the vine fully shoots. Hanging on the end of each trimmed cane is often a small drop of sap. In the low-lined morning light these drops reflect like diamonds, a sure sign that spring is at hand and the sap is once again flowing in the vines.

Like branches on the vine, it is not enough that we are just near the presence of Jesus, we must be connected to him in a way that nourishes our lives. We are not transformed by just having read the Bible, praying or finding fellowship, but only to the extent that those things have helped us experience a growing relationship with Jesus in a way that allows his life flow into ours. How does that happen? He promised that if we remained in him his words would remain in us. In other words, if we live our lives in him, he will continue to speak to our hearts and show us more about himself and his Father's work.

Your closest friends know the most about you and vice versa. The better you know them the more accurately you understand their words and actions. At the beginning, Jesus told the disciples that they were clean, or freshly pruned, by the words he'd spoken to them. At the end he told them that his words of revelation define the nature of their relationship. He didn't want them to be his servants, but his friends:

> *"I no longer call you servants, because a servant does not know his master's business. Instead, I have called you friends, for everything that I learned from my Father I have made known to you."* — JOHN 15:15

There are three important ways this revelation takes place in our lives. The first should be most obvious—Scripture itself. Those who desire to be linked to the vine will be students of Scripture. Here is God's full revelation, recorded so that at any moment we can pick it up and know who he is and what he is doing in our lives.

Like worship, this is one of those places where Jesus has clearly invested his presence. If we want God's fullness of joy and fruitfulness, we will cultivate a regular feeding pattern from the stories of Scripture. We will come to learn how to read it, reflect on it, and interpret it accurately. Even Jesus used the power of Scripture to turn back the temptations of Satan.

However, the "words" Jesus referred to that night with his disciples are not completely fulfilled by Scripture alone. Learning to recognize his voice is a critical ingredient in our ability to enjoy the full glory of our friendship with him.

He delights in making himself known to his people and leading them in his ways. He has a long history of doing exactly that, from his personal appearances to Enoch, Noah, Abraham, and others, to the revelation of his law and his counsel through his prophets. Finally, God spoke again in the greatest revelation of all—his own Son, the exact representation of God himself. Did God's revealing nature end there? It did not.

Jesus himself told his disciples just after his tale of the vineyard that he had much more to tell them. But because they were unable to hear it he entrusted that revelation to the work of the Holy Spirit (John 16:12). He would guide them into all truth.

Jesus wanted his disciples to know that they wouldn't have to go on alone, trying to make do with the best applications of all he had said to them. When the Holy Spirit came on the day of Pentecost, it was the fulfillment of God's promise to reveal himself to all who follow him. The result, demonstrated throughout the early church, was a people empowered by God's presence and sensitive to his voice. This promise was extended to everyone the Father would call to himself from then on (Acts 2:39). God's activity on our behalf didn't end with Scripture's completion. His revelation continues even to the present.

Silent gods are false gods. People prefer them because they would rather follow their own idea of a god than serve the awesome, transcendent God of the ages. To embrace God's revealing nature, however, doesn't devalue Scripture one bit. In fact, it does just the opposite. Scripture is the complete revelation of all that God is and all that he comes to do on behalf of men. Anything the Spirit speaks today will only apply the truths of Scripture to the immediacy of our needs.

Scripture also helps us develop sensitivity to God's voice by recognizing the things he says and does. These are God's words absolutely, and learning to hear him there will help us recognize his thoughts when he breathes them into our hearts. Measuring our impressions against Scripture is also the only objective test we have to distinguish the difference between our thoughts and God's.

Paul the apostle warned us that our perception of God's voice in this life would not come with absolute clarity. He compared it to a poor reflection in a mirror (1 Corinthians 13:12). Though it is still a valuable vantage point, we have to recognize that we will not see perfectly until we are transformed at his coming. If our perceptions of God's voice don't square with Scripture, whether in content or intent, they can be soundly rejected. God will never act in a way that violates what he's already revealed about himself.

The friendship Jesus offered his followers hinges on intimate communication. Jesus wants you to know what the Father is doing in your life and in situations around you. He doesn't want you to grope around in uncertainty, and so he has offered you his ever-present voice.

Sometimes, however, despite our best efforts in prayer or study, we remain confused, unsure of the Father's will for us. We usually cycle through feelings of condemnation that he isn't being clear with us because we've done something wrong, to anger that he is holding back on us, to the mistaken conclusion that God doesn't speak today.

I can't tell you why at times it is more difficult to hear Jesus' voice. I do know he's promised to disclose to us what the Father is doing so that we don't have to guess what he's up to or resign ourselves to fatalism. Developing this discernment is a lifelong venture for a branch. I've no doubt God speaks to all of his followers daily. We just don't always recognize his voice. It is easily drowned out by the clamor of our environment, our fears, or our own desires.

Finally, God makes himself known in real conversations with other believers. I find many things are clarified in my heart as I share them with others who are as passionate for Jesus as I am. That can also cross centuries by reading the words of those who have illuminated the ways of Jesus before us.

Studying the Scriptures, learning to listen to his voice, and fellowshipping with other believers work together. We don't have to discard any one of them in deference to another. When all three of them bring the same insight into focus, we can have some measure of confidence in the way God is leading us.

Remaining in his words allows our relationship with him to grow and will nourish us to live through the summer seasons of our life with his wisdom and resource.

Chapter 21

Enemies of Maturity

That Satan might not outwit us.
For we are not unaware of his schemes.
2 CORINTHIANS 2:11

I've got four new young vines growing in my backyard. I planted them two years ago. Last summer when the grapes started to ripen I took my granddaughters out to let them taste some fresh-grown grapes. A few days later when they returned, I took them out again and found the vines had been stripped bare. Birds had eaten all of the grapes and there were none left for us to enjoy.

Forty years removed from my father's vineyard I forget how many enemies seek to destroy the grapes. Not only do birds steal them as they get ripe, but worm-like nematodes can attack the roots, mildew can rot the grapes, and insects can attack the leaves destroying their ability to sweeten the crop.

One year a group of black moths stole their way into my backyard and laid their eggs in some grapevines I had planted there. Days later the army hatched. Small yellow caterpillars with brilliant purple and black stripes fanned out across the leaves, devouring them as they moved.

Skeletonizers. Their name stirs up gruesome images. They leave behind only the veins of the leaves, eerie skeletons of life destroyed.

Though they are hardly the size of a pinhead when they hatch, their sheer numbers can quickly overwhelm a cane. In a few days they can reduce a beautifully arching cane of greenery into a vegetative graveyard. If I am not careful the war can be half over before I ever knew it began. The enemies of summer are numerous indeed and attack at every level of the branch's growth and development.

At the very times we are most stressed, as vines are in the heat of summer, Satan rushes in like a flood. He rarely launches one offensive, but attacks on many fronts at the same time. Often when I am helping someone through a crisis, he or she will run through a list of all that's going wrong at the moment: "Believe me, Wayne, I could handle any one of these things alone, but together they're just too much for me to handle."

Regretfully many who expect the joys of spring to last through harvest are left unprepared for the onslaught of conflict that summer brings. Very real enemies exist to our growing friendship with Jesus. Failure to recognize and deal with them will cause us to do exactly what the branches of a vine will do when they are stressed—cast off the fruit in hopes of preserving itself.

When we are discouraged by difficulties it is easy to give up and withdraw from him. The fruit God is growing will wither and summer will be for naught. Our friendship with Jesus is always in the enemy's sights as he looks for any way he can to dislodge our affection and attention from our Lord. In the parable of the sower, some of the seeds fell on soil that was covered with thorns. When the thorns, or weeds, grew up they choked out the new plants. *The one who received the seed that fell among the thorns is the man who hears the word, but the worries of this life and the deceitfulness of wealth choke it, making it unfruitful.* (Matthew 13:22)

Two weapons wage war against our friendship with Jesus. The first is the worries of life. That is why Jesus told us, "Do not worry!" God will take care of you when you look to him first and foremost. He wants to keep your friendship safe from the destruction that our anxieties cause. However, I don't often see believers take effective countermeasures against anxiety and stress. Many people seem to wear it as a merit badge of how difficult their life is.

How easily anxiety can take over our minds and make us blame God for not fixing the very thing we worry about! Almost all the seeds of doubt, unbelief, envy, and bitterness proceed from our worries. If we don't find our way into a real trust in God's love, we will be threatened by other believers who don't seem to have the same struggles we do.

Nothing good comes from anxiety. Ask Jesus to grow your trust in him enough to overwhelm those anxieties.

Satan's second weapon is the deceitfulness of wealth, whether we have money or not. If we seek wealth as the solution to our problems, greed will result. If we already have it, and most of us in the West do by worldwide standards, we risk becoming complacent and distracted by all it can buy or all the effort it takes to maintain it. Both destroy our friendship with Jesus.

Complacency is probably the greater danger because of its subtlety. Though it is the opposite of anxiety, it actually produces the same result. Wealth can make us so comfortable, so distracted, so convinced of its promise of security that its very existence threatens our need for God. Instead of seeking him desperately, we hold on to a safe piece of Christianity while we lose ourselves in the excessive luxuries and distractions that wealth offers.

God is not against legitimate enjoyments. He is only against us becoming so committed to our own amusement that we lose sight of him.

When that happens our trust in God is destroyed, and our friendship with him is subverted by lies. We end up trusting more in our comfort than in him. We may only come to see this deception when our wealth fails us. Like weeds, anxiety and wealth's deception need to be expunged wherever we find them.

But there are many other enemies as well. Selfish ambition and vain conceit are often mentioned in Scripture as incentives that will keep us from following him, undermining the work of summer to mature the fruit. Those who do not discover the joy and freedom of obedience will never bear fruit. The enemy will do all he can to impede that obedience with temptation and distraction.

We also give in to the enemy's devices when we give the place Jesus wants in our lives to another human being. Jeremiah warned his hearers: *Many shepherds will ruin my vineyard and trample down my field; they will turn my pleasant field into a desolate wasteland.* (Jeremiah 12:10)

Nothing can destroy fruitfulness faster than ungodly leadership— men and women who use positions of authority to manipulate and exploit people instead of serving their growth in Christ. This results partly from people who want to lord over others and partly from people who would rather follow a pastor, author, or other influential person than develop their own relationship with Jesus. We can't ignore this danger under the guise of preserving Christian unity. Bad leadership needs to be recognized and resisted. Don't allow anyone to curtail your own obedience to Jesus in the name of loyalty to a man or his institution. Rather find godly men and women whos hearts are more concerned for your fruitfulness, than their own. There you'll find leaders after God's heart.

Even the delay of summer itself can be an enemy to the promise God has put in our hearts: "He is delaying or he didn't really mean it after all." But God does not delay; every promise he has made he is actively working to fulfill even as you read this page. Too many people misunderstand that fact. He doesn't always work quickly because he is doing a deep work in our hearts. If you can only see the fruit when it finally matures, you will have a miserable time in God's vineyard. From the day he promises to do something, God is at work to fulfill that promise. Don't let the enemy trick you into thinking otherwise, or you will grow frustrated with God and cast off the ripening fruit before it matures.

As the fruit begins to ripen, the enemy launches a full frontal assault to destroy it. The betrayal of a friend or disappointed expectations in other believers can create anger and bitterness that eats away at the sweetness he wants to produce in us. Instead of growing in love we become jaded or cynical. The enemy will even bring up old hurts from the past to rob us of the desire to respond with his love to people around us.

In almost every case the answer is simply to turn again toward him and embrace the joy of his work in us. There is no weakness we have greater than he, no mistake we've made that is bigger than he, and no enemy of our souls that will prevail against his presence in our lives if we just keep coming back to him and letting him have his way in us.

Chapter 22

The Farmer's Diligence

*I went past the field of the sluggard, past the vineyard of the man
who lacks judgment; thorns had come up everywhere, the ground was
covered with weeds, and the stone-wall was in ruins.*

PROVERBS 24:30–31

Summer in the vineyard is an all-out war. It may not look
that way to the casual observer who drives by on a summer day—
the vines may look content sitting out in the afternoon sun. But,
as we've seen, looks can be deceiving. Fruitfulness is a process
laced with conflict.

For the farmer, bringing a crop to fruitfulness is a never-ending
struggle against destructive forces. Farming is not like writing
a book; you don't spend a few years of diligent effort, achieve a
finished project, and look back on it for years to come. Farming
is doing the same tasks year in and year out, repeated again and
again.

One moment after the farmer plows the weeds down in a row
of vines, new ones begin to grow. They too will have to be cut. As
soon as a pest is expunged from the field, its cousins are already
infiltrating. The wilderness will forever seek to reclaim the land
taken from it.

Neglect in the kingdom of God is not a mere delay in our
spiritual growth; it is an act of destruction. There is no such thing

as standing still in the life of God. If you are not growing you are withering.

One of the ways that farmers check the health of their vineyard is to look at the new leaves emerging at the end of each cane. That growth doesn't stop at the end of spring; it continues to the last days of harvest. If the growth stops or looks weak, the farmer knows something is wrong. Either the field is too dry, or needs fertilizer, or is being weakened by pests.

Periodically, especially in difficult times, I'll have a conversation with God about my own spiritual journey. Am I gaining fresh insights into his character and wisdom? Am I finding ways to let him love me so that my trust in him is growing? Am I finding opportunities to love others in ways that make him known? If not, I usually find I've grown complacent or neglectful as the demands of the world have eaten away at my relationship with him. This gives me a chance to refocus my eyes on him.

When I have my eyes on him, I can rest assured that he is having his way in me—even if I don't see the immediate fulfillment of his promises. The Father is a diligent caretaker in the vineyard. He will do what needs to be done, when it needs to be done. Good farming is not convenient.

My father got up at 5:30 in the morning to sulfur his grapevines before the winds came up. I'm sure he would much rather have done it at 10:00, but it can't be done then, at least not effectively. Many times I've seen him leave a party he was hosting at his own home, put on his work clothes, and go out to check his irrigation. When it's time to water, you can't wait just because it is the Fourth of July or the day of the family reunion. When the water is running, it has to be checked even if you have other things you'd prefer to do.

Tending to our spiritual nature isn't always convenient either. Spiritual life is real. It needs to be tended to when it needs to be tended to. For people that work eight-to-five jobs and compartmentalize their lives into work, recreation, and family, this may be difficult to grasp. But having grown up on a farm, I understand it very well.

We need to follow the Spirit's leading for what is needed each day. This rarely fits effortlessly into my schedule. There may even be some cost in it and it may force me to make some difficult choices. We might have to say no to something good to embrace a greater grace.

Watching my father tend his vineyard taught me this valuable lesson. Some weeks of the year he had to put in twelve to fourteen hour days to get the work done that needed doing. At other times the vineyard's demands would be light and he would rest in what he'd already done.

God is our caretaker. He is always on the lookout for those things that will encourage our growth and mitigate the destructive influence of the enemy. As we diligently look to him he will give us whatever we need to draw from his grace and to overcome the enemy's attempts to discourage or distract us. By following his lead we can recognize those attitudes or the busyness that draws us away from him.

Diligence is only doing what the Spirit wants you to do every day, without excuse or delay because it might be inconvenient. Don't mistake this diligence for busyness, thinking that an abundance of religious activity will stir fruitfulness. It will not. And don't mistake it for legalism—assuming you can earn fruitfulness by your performance.

Much of the farmer's work along these lines is not spectacular. It won't draw the acclaim of crowds or win achievement awards. It's the mundane work of shoveling weeds, tying up canes, or repairing broken wires. It's the kind of work that needs to be done again and again to bring the vineyard to fruitfulness.

The same is true of our spirituality. Don't seek the spirituality that is seen by others—visible spirituality will not bring you into freedom and fruitfulness. Instead be intentional about Jesus' work in your life. If you don't, you will be easily distracted by everything else going on around you. Years will go by without you ever seeing a harvest of his fruit and you'll wonder why. Sadly, it is very easy to sacrifice unwittingly our spiritual growth to take the easy road or satisfy the whims of our own appetites.

Only the Father's diligence can help us beyond that. And learning to follow him will soon make the spiritual realities around us far more significant than the mundane world we live in.

Chapter 23
Having Done All, Stand!

after you have done everything stand.
EPHESIANS 6:13

The summer comes slowly to an end. We're only two weeks away from the harvest now. The vineyard is in its final stages of production. The fruit is ripening, making measurable gains in sugar content every day.

Where would you imagine the farmer to be in the most critical days before the harvest? Vigilantly prowling his fields? Battling the unending armies of insects or weeds? Fretting over what unseen trouble may be lurking out there to destroy his harvest? Hardly.

I'll tell you where my family was in the beginning weeks of August: We went camping.

Unbelievable, isn't it? But there really wasn't anything for Dad to do in those last few weeks. The groundwork had already been laid. Whatever he hadn't done before this moment wasn't going to make a difference anyway. The field was watered and the vines were sulfured to keep out the mildew. It was too late to spray for insects, since the insecticide would only hurt the fruit. No weed can grow tall enough in two weeks to challenge the vine. At this time the fruit is going to ripen no matter what you do. So we went on vacation.

One of the things a good farmer has a firm grasp of is where his work ends and where God's begins. A farmer can only do so much. He can water, cultivate, fertilize, and prune, but he cannot make anything grow—not one bunch of grapes, not even a leaf. Only God does that.

Jesus told a parable about wheat that illustrates this point perfectly and encourages us to live similarly:

> *This is what the kingdom of God is like. A man scatters seed on the ground. Night and day, whether he sleeps or gets up, the seed sprouts and grows, though he does not know how. All by itself the soil produces grain–first the stalk, then the head, then the full kernel in the head. As soon as the grain is ripe, he puts the sickle to it, because the harvest has come.*
>
> — MARK 4:26–29

We can sow and we can reap, but we cannot make one thing grow. To know the peace of God even in the most difficult of times, we have to know where our responsibilities begin and where they end.

We don't make things grow and we're not responsible for results: God is. Discover that fact and you'll have found the secret to the Lord's peace. All we need to do is obey Jesus, and God will see to it that his purposes are accomplished.

The best farmers are patient farmers. A farmer who works the land near my home is not so patient. He is always working his ground with one implement or another. Going over the field dozens of times when a few trips would suffice, he adds greatly to his cost of operation. Last year he planted his cotton too early, and a late spring rain forced him to plant the whole field all over again. He's young; he'll learn.

My father is the most patient man I know. Whether being a farmer produced this in him, or whether he chose farming because it fit his temperament, I don't know. But my father has a keen sense of what is his responsibility and what is God's. And he flatly refuses to try to fulfill God's.

When the rains came and destroyed his crop one harvest, his faith in God never flinched. I would have lain awake at night fretting, pacing the patio rebuking the storm, screaming at God in case he had forgotten me under the cloud cover. But I never saw my dad do any such thing. I'm sure he didn't enjoy seeing a year's worth of labor wiped out in a few hours, but he didn't get angry or shake his fist at God. Instead he threw up his hands, cocked his head with a smile that revealed the inner peace that guides his life, and said, "What else can I do?"

We can sow and reap, but only God gives the increase. You learn that in a vineyard. City life reinforces the ridiculous notion that if things aren't going our way it's because we aren't trying hard enough. When you work with growing things you have to be patient. You have to do your part but you also realize that the most important work will come from God. We can't expect God to plant or weed, since he asked us to do that but he is the one who makes the branch grow and the fruit ripen.

Whenever I read Ephesians 6, I think of those August vacations. "After you have done everything stand!" When you've done everything you know to do, rest. Even when problems remain unresolved let him complete his work on his timetable.

Any reliance on our efforts above his will only spoil the harvest. I see too many people at the very threshold of the promises God has made to them who just can't wait until the final work is done. Like Abraham getting Sarah's handmaiden pregnant because he'd lost hope in the promise, they try to do by human strength what only God can do to fulfill his promise. They try some substitute only to discover later that it falls far short of God's promise and only creates more problems.

When we try to possess for ourselves the promises of God, we will grow increasingly frustrated. Only God makes things grow. We need only to trust his plans and then be patient.

Be patient, then, brothers, until the Lord's coming. See how the farmer waits for the land to yield its valuable crop and how patient he is for the autumn and spring rains. You too, be patient and stand firm, because the Lord's coming is near.

— JAMES 5:7,8

Chapter 24

Softer and Sweeter

Take my yoke upon you and learn from me,
for I am gentle and humble in heart, and you will find rest
for your souls.
MATTHEW 11:29

In the last few weeks before harvest the grapes ripen rapidly. Two dramatic changes take place in these final weeks to make them the succulent grapes the farmer desires.

By early August the grapes have grown almost to full size. But if you pick one and bite into it then, you'll be greatly disappointed. The grapes are still hard, and tart enough to pucker your lips. It is during these final weeks before harvest that the grapes fill up with sugar, making them soft and sweet.

The leaves are in full production at this time, pumping the grape bunches full of sugar. Almost daily you can taste the changing sweetness as the sugar content soars. This influx of sugar also softens the pulp inside the grape. As you bite through the firm outer skin, you'll find the pulp has softened inside so it almost explodes in your mouth.

When the grapes turn soft and sweet, harvest is at hand. Today with special instruments farmers can measure the sugar content and know exactly when the grapes are fully ripe. Farmers of old, however, trusted their eyes and taste buds to tell them the same thing.

Softer and sweeter. The same things that signal the maturity of a grape also signal the maturity of a believer. As God brings his promises to completion in our lives, one of the signs that he is about finished is the softness and sweetness that floods our demeanor. Earlier, in the midst of promise and warfare, we might find ourselves a bit harder, full of arrogance, fighting and striving in our own efforts to accomplish God's work. But the perseverance of summer shows the weakness of our own efforts.

By learning to trust God's doing more than our own we become softened with humility and gentleness and sweetened with loving-kindness. All of the fruits of the spirit—love, joy, peace, patience, kindness, goodness, faithfulness, gentleness, and self-control—are expressions of a life that has been through the fire and come through with greater trust in the Father's affection and his work in the world.

However, these are not the attributes most desired or generated by the world system. If you want to make it in this world, you have to be tough. Don't show any sign of weakness (meaning kindness or goodness) because someone is waiting to take advantage of you the moment you do. Those are the rules. Everyone who succeeds learns them early and follows them adamantly.

Everyone, that is, except Jesus. In every conflict he faced, through every lie directed against him by those who sought to destroy him, he only demonstrated these incredible fruits of the Spirit.

His authority scared many people, even though he held no political power or ever enforced his will on anyone. He went about doing good, but this only threatened those who would not allow God access to their lives. "We've never seen anyone like this!" the people gasped as they looked for ways to kill him.

Softness is not weakness; in God's kingdom it is the greatest measure of strength.

All too often I've seen people loaded with knowledge and zeal but still captives of the world's system. They are harsh and their words are judgmental. In their wake are a lot of offended people—not by the gospel—but by the way they've been treated.

They want to be somebody. But as long as they want to be

somebody their ministry will be polluted. Even in places where God has genuinely called them they are defensive and easily threatened, and they compensate for that with aggression and manipulation. Where they don't succeed, they are frustrated and bitter at those they perceive as impeding on their ministries.

Those who have lived deeply in Jesus reflect the same humility and gentleness that Jesus did. They no longer advance their own agenda, angry when they don't get what they think God has for them. They are not pushovers because they will resolutely stand in the truth, and they do so with a grace for others. They don't threaten to leave and go somewhere else "where their gifts will be appreciated." They easily express the compassion and care of Father to those around them. With simple love and concern they are able to help people engage God. They know that God opens doors and shuts them, and when he does, no man stands in his way. They are content with their part and have no need to diminish others to make the light shine brighter on them.

Living in that reality shows us that the harvest is at hand. If we don't live in that place, our misplaced passion can easily crush the very people we're called to touch with his life.

The end product of summer, for those who traverse it with perseverance and growing trust, is a gentle and humble spirit. There is no more accurate sign of maturity than those who treat others, *all* others, with kindness and gentleness. When that settles on your heart, you know that summer has come to an end.

Let the harvest begin!

Fall

Harvest Time

Let us not become weary in doing good,
for at the proper time we will reap a harvest
if we do not give up.
GALATIANS 6:9

Fortunately summer does not last forever. Eventually the days grow shorter, the heat less intense, and one taste of the grapes confirms that they are now sweet enough for the harvest.

Chapter 25
The Joys of Harvest

*Those who harvest it will eat it and praise the Lord,
and those who gather the grapes will drink it in the courts
of my sanctuary.*
ISAIAH 62:9

To the grape farmer there is no scene more awe-inspiring than swollen grape bunches cascading out of the leaves like a billowing fountain. All his effort during the past year was aimed toward this moment.

The vine sags under the weight of the fruit like a tired, swaybacked horse. The leaves are ragged and frayed, dulled by a heavy cloak of dust. Some have yellowed and others have wilted completely. Many have pieces ripped away, remnants of summer's warfare.

Though scarred and bruised, the vines emerge laden with fruit. The farmer cherishes the vines because they have completed their work and are full of the desired grapes. Their purpose was never to look good—only to produce fruit.

The vineyard uses the entire growing season to develop and ripen its fruit. As the approaching fall brings cooler temperatures and shorter days, the grapes bulge with sweetness. The farmer waits until the sugar content is high enough to suit his purpose, and then he sets the knife to the field to garner the grapes.

Farmers have no way to measure their success weekly, or even monthly. Their labor is directed toward one small span of time when the harvest is gathered. These are days of great joy. Depending on the farmer, he may gather the grape bunches directly for use as table grapes, or process them into wine, or (as in my father's case) lay them on the ground in the sun to dry as raisins. Scripture makes reference to all three uses.

As much as I hated farm work as a child, some of my sweetest memories include the last ride on the tractor into the barn. The sun-ripened raisins formed a mountain as they sloped down to the edges of the box.

The crop was in. We had beaten the winter storms for another year, and now the crop was safe. The hot, dusty work was over. I remember on more than one occasion surveying the awesome sight of row upon row of boxes stretched out across the top of the hill where the outbuildings on my father's farm stood. A year's worth of labor and all of my father's income for an entire year sat beneath the black plastic covering the boxes.

The last act of harvest was always a celebration. Shouts of joy, song, and laughter filled the air on that final ride home. Afterward we would clean up and go out to eat a feast—even if it was a late dinner at Denny's—to celebrate the harvest and the gracious God who made it possible.

I suspect that the final harvest in the kingdom of God will be like that. Paul speaks in 2 Timothy 4 of his departure to the Father and the joy that awaits him in God's presence. Revelation tells of a marriage banquet where we will sit down with the King and feast in his presence. What a great day that will be for all who have been faithful!

But like the vine, we have not been shaped for only one harvest. There are many seasons in our spiritual journeys when the fruits of our labors are rewarded and we get to see the result of the Father's work in us. These too are days full of celebration. And they are often days of learning to understand why God didn't always intervene in our circumstances the way we thought he might. He was producing something far better than our own temporal conveniences would ever allow. While we seek personal comfort or happiness, God is far more focused on the ultimate freedom that comes from conforming us to the image of his Son. Remember, this is his work, not ours. He is ultimately the victor and we are his prize.

This is worship in its highest form. God knows no greater joy than to receive the fruitfulness of his sons and daughters.

Chapter 26

Out of Water, Wine!

Celebrate the Feast of Harvest with the first fruits
of the crops you sow in your field.
Celebrate the Feast of Ingathering at the end of the year,
when you gather in your crops from the field.
EXODUS 23:16

The wedding was over. The feast to celebrate it was in full swing. The joyful sounds of animated conversation and dancing filled the room. So far everything was going well but it did not look like it was going to continue. Disaster lurked in the wings and was about to come center stage. The groom had not ordered enough wine for his guests, and it had run out before they had.

This would set the stage for Jesus' first miracle: A party was about to die. Even though this was an embarrassing social blunder, as far as needs go I wouldn't rate it very high on a significance scale. Surely the need here was not as great as Mary's brother dying, or of being caught in a raging midnight storm on the Sea of Galilee.

Jesus told the stewards to fill the washing pots to the brim and take some to the master of the banquet. They did so, and found out that somewhere between the time they had filled the pots and when their contents were tasted by the master of the banquet, it had been changed into wine—better wine than had been used earlier.

Those that knew how the wine came to be there were awestruck by the miracle. But most at the party hadn't paid enough attention to recognize it. Yet the man who recorded the event had, and he told us that on the basis of this miracle the disciples put their faith in Jesus.

Out of water he made wine! That he did it should not be significant. As C.S. Lewis pointed out in an essay on miracles in *God in the Dock*, this was something he had done many times before:

> *God creates the vine and teaches it to draw up water by its roots, and, with the aid of the sun, to turn that water into a juice, which will ferment and take on certain qualities. Thus every year, from Noah's time till ours, God turns water into wine. That, men fail to see.*

What was significant this time is that Jesus did in a moment what he normally does over an entire growing season.

This is the Lord of the Harvest, who made himself known at a wedding feast. Lewis goes on to draw a powerful point: If such miracles only convince us that Christ is God, they have only done half their work. Miracles are "a retelling in small letters of the very same story, which is written across the whole world in letters too large for some to see." Thus this miracle only has its full impact "if whenever we see a vineyard or drink a glass of wine we remember that here works he who sat at the wedding party in Cana."

Not surprisingly, harvest and joy are closely connected throughout Scripture. In an agrarian society that predated cold storage and prepackaged food, the harvest was a lifeline. The previous year's food would be running low, paced to last through the year. That may not be easy for us to grasp with adequate fervor when our supermarkets are loaded with food every day of the year. How can we recognize the vulnerability of the harvest when we can replace the freeze-devastated citrus crop of California by shipping in oranges from Florida, or vice versa?

For a society without those luxuries, the harvest was a genuine time of thanksgiving and celebration—two celebrations in particular. The Feast of Harvest came at the beginning as precious first fruits were offered to God in thankfulness for another crop. The Feast of

Ingathering marked the successful completion of the harvest itself. Both were to be celebrated before God. He, not nature, had provided bountifully for the year to come.

Out of our broken lives God brings forth the fruit of his kingdom in us and it is certainly a cause for celebration. Maybe that's why God chose a vineyard to represent our spiritual growth. Even the fruit of the vineyard speaks of joy.

Grapes and raisins were desired treats in days prior to chocolate cake and ice cream. They not only provided nourishment but also offered a sweet contrast to the harsher grains and meat that made up most of the population's diet. Remember how awed the Israelites were when their spies in Canaan brought back grape bunches that had to be carried on poles because they were too large to carry by hand?

Wine is the most-used scriptural symbol for joy. When Solomon expressed his delight in the Lord he exalted it above wine, evidently the standard by which other things desirable were measured: *We rejoice and delight in you; we will praise your love more than wine.* (Song of Songs 1:4)

When God gave instructions to the Israelites about using their tithe, wine and celebration were a big part of it: *Use the silver to buy whatever you like: cattle, sheep, wine or other fermented drink, or anything you wish. Then you and your household shall eat there in the presence of the Lord your God and rejoice.* (Deuteronomy 14:26)

I realize that these uses of wine are confusing for many of us today. The church I grew up in found it inconceivable that Jesus would go to a wedding to change water into wine. (Most of them would have gone to a wedding party to turn wine back into water!) We even defined wine as unfermented grape juice. I grew up thinking the Greek word for wine was *Welch's*.

To this day I am a teetotaler, though less for conscience than for unappreciative taste buds. But I am familiar with the devastation alcohol consumption can foist on our society. A drunk driver killed one of the friends I grew up with while he was in his first year of college. I have counseled too many people who were the victims of alcoholic parents and too many who themselves battle its temptation.

Scripture is not oblivious to this dark side of wine. Though it was a drink to be shared with joy at celebrations, drunkenness is resoundingly condemned throughout Scripture. Proverbs tells us that wine destroys those who give themselves over to its power. They will end in poverty and shame. Wine is even used as a symbol of the last great evil civilization that will fill our world: *Fallen! Fallen is Babylon the Great, which made all the nations drink the maddening wine of her adulteries.* (Revelation 14:8)

The reason wine makes a powerful symbol of the joy and freedom that God wants to bring to his people is that, like all his other gifts (ministry, food, sex), it has the potential for our enjoyment or our destruction. What makes the difference is whether we partake of these things as gifts God has given, or whether we spend them on our own pleasure, using them as substitutes for God.

We are exhorted to let God alone be our source of help through any pain or trial. Thus wine can be a symbol of either the enemy's work or of God's. Perhaps no Scripture brings that together as well as Ephesians 5:18: *Do not get drunk on wine, which leads to debauchery. Instead, be filled with the Spirit.*

Wine is only a *symbol* of the joy and celebration that come from his presence.

That's why Paul tells us not to be drunk with wine like the world, but filled with the Spirit. He alone is the source of enduring joy. Thus wine is also linked to the Holy Spirit as well as to joy. He is the new wine, and we are encouraged to drink freely and often from his fountain.

Celebration and joy are major themes at harvest time. Even though it was purchased by the pain and toil of summer, the celebration of the harvest overruns our suffering. There is even a hint of that fact at the last meal that Jesus shared with his disciples.

What a confusing night for his men. He talked of his impending departure as they shared the Passover meal! As they ate, he talked of his body broken and his blood shed. They were confused and afraid. What kind of ordeal was he describing? When Jesus spoke of his dying he took the cup in his hand. A cup of wine! Previous to that moment there was nothing in the Passover making wine a symbol of blood. There was no need to, for the blood was smeared on the doorposts from the sacrifice. The unleavened bread and bitter herbs were to remind them of their slavery. This was not the time for pained recollection, but a time of celebration with thanksgiving that God had passed over them and spared their lives and would take them out of Egypt. And the celebration was in the wine.

So he took the cup. "This cup is the new covenant in my blood, which is poured out for you." Pain and celebration are brought together in the fruit of the vine. As we begin our own seasons of harvest, we can remember whose blood makes it possible, and celebrate his love for us.

It was at this meal with his disciples that Jesus vested in the wine the symbol of his sacrifice. The very cup that symbolized celebration even in the midst of tragedy would carry that symbol into the New Covenant. Jesus didn't want us looking back at the cross with gruesome anguish; this was to be a cup of celebration. The blood had been shed and the work of redemption was complete at great pain, but resulted in even greater joy.

Chapter 27

Whatever I Ask?

If you remain in me and my words remain in you,
ask whatever you wish, and it will be given you.
JOHN 15:7

It never happened in my earthly father's vineyard.

Not once did any of the branches ask us for anything. We cared for them and they quietly went along. Jesus told his disciples that it wasn't that way in his vineyard. In his vineyard the branches get to make requests of the Father with the anticipation that he will give them whatever they ask. Amazing!

One of the qualities of friendship Jesus offered his disciples was to make requests of his Father. It reveals yet another place where we go to remain in his presence—prayer. Not only does he want to speak to us, but he also invites us to speak to him. This makes our engagements with him in prayer a fresh and active exchange. The Almighty God who spoke worlds into existence invites you to ask whatever you wish from him with the promise that he will give it.

Regretfully, however, instead of being awed by this promise, we are often frustrated by it. Such a promise is only valuable if God actually backs it up, and most believers have a backlog of unanswered prayers that seems to make a mockery of it.

Whatever we ask for we can have? Who is he trying to fool?

One morning I read that promise to my children as part of our breakfast devotions. When I got done reading it, Andy, my ten-year-old son (who rarely made comments about anything from the Bible), immediately responded, "Well, that isn't true." His tone wasn't accusing or frustrated, just matter-of-fact.

"What do you mean?"

"What you just read: It doesn't really happen."

I was sure what he meant, but I asked him which part anyway so I could hear from his own lips what lurked in his young mind.

"It says whatever you wish for you can have. I wished for a big-screen TV and I don't have one." Case closed.

"It doesn't say we can have what we wish for, but what we ask for. Have you ever asked for one?" Don't worry; I knew I was on thin ice here.

"Dad, can I have a big-screen TV?"

"It doesn't say to ask me," I answered, and then asked Andy if he had ever prayed about this, and he honestly said he hadn't. Then we talked about whether we should ask God for something like that, and his response was, "It says 'whatever you ask . . .' "

I'll grant you that the promise Jesus makes in this passage appears all-inclusive. At face value it suggests a 100 percent return on any request we make. Who, however, has an answered prayer list that reflects that standard of success?

How easy it is to overlook all the times God has answered our prayers when our latest request is seemingly on the back burner. It is no wonder people eventually give up on prayer, either convinced that God doesn't really answer prayers today or at least won't for someone like them.

Our prayer theology is finally reduced to nothing more than throwing up a request and hoping for the best, like filling out a requisition form. Ship it upstairs and maybe if you're good enough, or if your request is pure enough, you might get what you ask for. But most times you won't, so don't expect too much. After all, God knows what's best.

On the surface, such thinking sounds wonderfully biblical and wholly submitted to the Master's desires, but it flies in the face of the very certainty about our prayers that Jesus put forth to the branches in his vineyard. There is a place in him, he said, where we can ask for anything and know that the Father will give it to us.

Don't let the disappointments and imperfections of the past rob you of this hope and subsequently short-circuit the process for getting there. Like almost every other promise in Scripture, it is not intended to frustrate you but designed to stimulate your growth until it is fulfilled.

For Jesus' promise of answered prayer has a clear precondition. We can have whatever we ask, "if," as he already said, "you remain in me and my words remain in you." If we're drawing our life from him, and allowing his words to have access to every corner of our lives, then we can anticipate him answering our prayers.

One of the things that most baffles me is when believers miss this connection between intimate relationship and answered prayer. Something far deeper is at stake when we learn to remain in him and his words. By staying close enough to Jesus to know what he desires, we will find our desires being transformed to match his.

In C. S. Lewis' fourth book of the Narnia series, *The Silver Chair*, Prince Caspian arrives in heaven and expresses one of his desires to Aslan, the Christ-symbol. "Is that wrong?" he asked.

"You cannot want wrong things anymore, now that you have died, my son!"

We can experience that same reality here as we die to our own desires. Jesus wants us to find a place in prayer where every request can be answered, because every request is a godly one aligned with his will. It is impossible for us to remain in him and use prayer for our own gain or convenience. Not only do ill-gotten prayers reinforce our selfish motives, answering them just isn't possible from God's perspective.

What if God only let it rain in the San Joaquin Valley when someone prayed for it? That would be fine if there were just one person to contend with, but when you add many people, who would he listen to? No matter when it rains in our part of the San Joaquin Valley, someone's crop is hurt by it. During our recent five-year drought we had what our media termed a "Miracle March." Seven inches of rain fell in that month, almost two-thirds of our normal yearly total.

As elated as most people were, the media was still able to find farmers who suffered from the rain. Fruit trees with tender blossoms were most at risk. Some trees the hail stripped, while others couldn't be pollinated normally because the bees were grounded in the inclement weather. Cotton farmers lamented that they couldn't get into the fields to plant.

Regardless of what happened, some people would be overjoyed that their prayers were answered because they got what they wanted, while those who didn't would wonder why God doesn't love them.

Scripture gives many other reasons why our prayers go unanswered, and it is well for us to search them out. They are not intended to rob us of the certainty of God answering our prayers. Rather they are intended to show us why he sometimes doesn't, so that we can learn to pray for things that further his work in our lives.

When Jesus promised his disciples around that grapevine that he wanted to answer whatever request they would make of him, his purpose was not centered in them at all, but in God and his mission: *This is to my Father's glory, that you bear much fruit, showing yourselves to be my disciples.* (John 15:8)

God moving in response to our prayers brings glory to the Father. When God's power moves in our lives beyond our own abilities or plans, it testifies to his presence. People's attentions are drawn to the Father and not to our own skills.

God's answers are also a key ingredient to our bearing fruit. Developing an intimate relationship with the vine demands confidence that we can draw from him what we need. Without that active involvement we won't be able to produce anything fruitful in his kingdom, any more than a branch can produce fruit if it doesn't receive nourishment consistently from the vine. This also hints at the direction of our prayers. Instead of praying for God to save us out of difficult circumstances we will instead pray for that which will bring the greatest glory to God, which as we said earlier will produce in us the fruits of his Spirit.

His answers demonstrate an intimacy of friendship that testifies to God's reality in our lives and gives others hope of finding the same relationship as well. How often the disciples were enamored by Jesus' prayers! They could see how the Father immediately responded to his requests for a storm stilled, blind eyes healed, and sinful people forgiven.

"Teach us to pray" did not express a desire to learn a spiritual discipline, but to find out how to effectively connect with the Father. They wanted that same relationship, and so will others as they see him at work in us.

For all these reasons God wants to respond to our prayers with complete fulfillment, even more than we want him to. When he doesn't, this should be a signal to us that perhaps our request was wrong or that some wrong motives have twisted their way into our prayer. If we don't go on to probe why the prayer was not answered, we'll never become more effective in prayer and merely consign ourselves to sending requests and settling for whatever we're fortunate enough to get along the way. In the same way we should never get smug about the prayers he does answer, as if we in our goodness somehow deserve them.

Nothing we've covered in this chapter is intended to communicate that answered prayers are merit badges for our performance. God wants to teach us through our prayers how to zero in on his will, and how to bring it into reality through prayer. His goal is unchanged: He wants to give us whatever we ask. And if we'll remain in him he will teach us how and what to ask. It's one of the lessons he wants all of his branches to learn well.

Chapter 28
The Fruit Tells All

Do people pick grapes from thornbushes, or figs from thistles?
MATTHEW 7:16

For a period of about four to five years during my early teens, my father's vineyard didn't look as well cared for as it does today. Even the neighbors noticed. The weeds grew taller, the pests multiplied, and the long-term maintenance needs of the vineyard were neglected.

You might call this my father's fanatic stage. There was a fresh renewal going on in his spiritual life, and he was more excited about the things of God than I had ever seen him. He was always rushing off to a prayer meeting or conference, or helping someone in need. Many Christians at that time were certain that Jesus' second coming would happen before we ever reached the seventies.

In that spiritual climate the vineyard just didn't seem all that appropriate. If irrigation or spraying for insects had to wait an extra week, that was too bad. We were involved in the business of God's kingdom; let God take care of the vineyard.

My dad looks back at that time with a glimmer of laughter in his eyes. He sees now the folly of thinking that to serve God with all one's heart means we have to neglect our responsibilities in this world. At the time, however, the toll it took on the vineyard was very real. Without proper care the vineyard was not fully fruitful. Make whatever excuses you like, but the proof was in the fruit itself. These were not well cared for vines.

Fruit doesn't lie. As we saw earlier, it is the overflow of the vine's life—the greater the overflow, the sweeter the fruit. As a branch joined to Jesus himself, we are part of the healthiest of all vines. If we have kept ourselves firmly rooted in him through the stress of summer, his life will overflow in us. If not well, his fruit doesn't lie either.

The proof of a branch's life is found in the harvest. Its diligence will reap an abundance of fruit, useful for the Master in extending his kingdom. But there is another side to the harvest, one that is not so joyful. For those who have not remained in him, harvest exposes that reality as well.

Worse yet, if we have only pretended to draw life from Christ, but have in fact resisted his work in us while we've served ourselves, our fruit will bear our own likeness and not God's. The fruit testifies to the source of the branch:

> *Their vine comes from the vine of Sodom and from the fields of Gomorrah. Their grapes are filled with poison, and their clusters with bitterness. Their wine is the venom of serpents, the deadly poison of cobras.*
> —DEUTERONOMY 32:32,33

Scripture views the harvest in both positive and negative terms. It demonstrates the quality of our lives, whether good or bad. Thus, harvest is used to talk of both the celebration of those who know him, and the toxicity of those who have only lived for themselves.

When Paul saw how easily the Galatian believers abandoned their growing relationship with Jesus for a religion of rules and rituals, he was deeply disturbed and challenged them in the harshest tone. Their religious activity, even pursued with the utmost of fervor, would not bear Jesus' fruit in their lives. They had given up the gospel of promise—which was no gospel at all.

He likened his desire for them become to a fruitful harvest in Christ to a woman in childbirth: *My dear children, for whom I am again in the pains of childbirth until Christ is formed in you.* (Galatians 4:19) Nothing expresses the power of ministry better than taking pains to insure that Christ is taking shape in the lives of those we're engaged with.

And nothing describes fruit better than those places where Christ's character is reflected in ours. Those who know him will yearn to be like him. And for us who learn to live in him, the struggle of summer allows his character to emerge in our own. He actually takes shape in us, and we find ourselves even in the extreme moments of life responding with the kindness, patience, love, and self-control that he demonstrated when he was here.

This is not people trying to live kindly, patiently, or lovingly. These simply become the natural responses of people who are growing to know Jesus. This kind of fruit is not produced overnight, but is borne out of a long process of growing to trust in his love, to listen to his voice, and to learn how he works in the world. And what an incredible process it is.

What I love about this process is that as Christ is formed in us we are hardly aware of it until we are suddenly caught in a difficult situation and find ourselves responding differently than we've ever responded before. Instead of reacting in anger, or seeking our own way, we're more relaxed and sensitive to what God is doing in our situation and find that in doing so we are more helpful to others.

Harvest time tells the tale. The fruit that has developed in the background now takes center stage. Now we can be seen for who we really are. That's why Jesus told us that the fruit borne at harvest reveals a lot about people. Though he warned us not to judge others, he did say that we had a responsibility not to be gullible to the counsel and ministry of those who don't belong to him.

He didn't want us to judge other peoples motives or to make assumptions because of their boasts or failures. He said to look at their fruit instead. Their fruit will tell for sure who they are on the inside:

Watch out for false prophets. They come to you in sheep's clothing, but inwardly they are ferocious wolves. By their fruit you will recognize them. Do people pick grapes from thornbushes . . . ? Likewise every good tree bears good fruit, but a bad tree bears bad fruit. A good tree cannot bear bad fruit, and a bad tree cannot bear good fruit. Every tree that does not bear good fruit is cut down and thrown into the fire. Thus, by their fruit you will recognize them.

— MATTHEW 7:15-20

For too long our qualifications for Christian ministry have focused on expertise, charisma, self-proclaimed anointing, or an ability to say what we want to hear. Jesus tells us to look elsewhere: to people's true character. How are they when they think no one is looking?

Jesus didn't mean that they have to be perfect. He meant that they need to bear his character in their attitude and demeanor in the simplest of human interactions with the people closest to them—spouses, children, business associates, etc. If they don't exemplify that character, Jesus warned us not to believe what they say either. If they get angry when confronted, or lie to cover up their sinfulness, or treat others harshly and with arrogance, they are wolves in sheep's clothing. They are only around for what they can get from the sheep—power, money, or even a sense of personal success.

Trust the fruit, Jesus said. Though a person may for a time be able to pretend some godly attribute for a brief season, in his weak and tired moments his real nature will slip out and be exposed. Only the fruit produced by God himself can withstand the heat of battle.

Grace can restore us to God's presence, and it can forgive our sins and offer us a fresh start, but grace will not produce fruit unless it leads us into a transforming relationship with him. It will not make up for the times when we have given in to the enemy's lies and aborted our own fruit to save ourselves in times of stress.

God's harvest may surprise us. The people we thought were

pursuing God because of their gifts, temporal success, or charming words may not turn out to be his followers at all.

> *Not everyone who says to me, "Lord, Lord," will enter the kingdom of heaven, but only he who does the will of my father who is in heaven. Many will say to me on that day, "Lord, Lord did we not prophesy in your name, and in your name drive out demons and perform many miracles?" Then I will tell them plainly, "I never knew you. Away from me, you evildoers!"*
> — MATTHEW 7:21-23

Fruit is not measured in the acts of power we participated in, the numbers of people we touched, nor the acclaim we received from others. In the end all of that is meaningless. Fruit is measured by the transformation of character that can only arise out of a meaningful relationship with Jesus.

Chapter 29
Look at the Fields!

They are ripe for harvest.
JOHN 4:35

You probably don't think much about it when you sink your teeth into a delicious bowl of fruit. As the sparkling sweetness explodes in your mouth it is too easy to forget that the fruit is also a seed. That is how plants multiply for future generations.

The earliest passages in Genesis tell us that God created fruit for this dual purpose: food to be eaten and seed to be sown. So it is with the fruit of our friendship with Jesus. Because unregenerate hearts cannot clearly see the invisible God, they often get their first reflection of him by what they see in our lives. As he shapes us into his image, that fruit will also demonstrate to others what God is like.

How will they know his love if they don't get to see it in the way we love them? How will they understand his gentleness and forgiveness unless I demonstrate it even beyond their failures? How will they know he is faithful unless I am faithful in my relationship to them?

The fruit of our lives has its greatest use in this age by demonstrating God's reality and nature to others. During days of harvest not only do we enjoy and celebrate what God has accomplished in us, but we also see God touch others through our lives. Harvest time is ministry time. It is the fruit of our lives reaped to insure a future harvest.

Harvest is a twofold analogy in Scripture. Not only does it refer to the fruit of transformed character in our lives, but from a different vantage point, it also refers to the unsaved as a ripened harvest, or those who have been prepared to meet the Lord. The demonstration of God's nature in us is the means by which God propagates the gospel. We are workers called into that field to make him known.

This is not a burdensome task to be met through a complicated evangelism program. This is something that people who have been changed by God can't help but do as they go about their day. Changed lives demonstrate to people the reality of God. There are always people around us ready to respond to God if they see him in us.

Jesus spoke from experience; he had just found one earlier that morning. He was passing through Samaria, tired from the journey. It was almost noon, and instead of going into town with his followers to find lunch, he sat down by an out-of-the-way well. Was he lying in wait for the conversation to come, or did he just take advantage of the moment? I suspect the former . . . but in either case, a Samaritan woman came to draw water.

Outside of town? In the heat of midday? Unusual. Everyone else had come earlier in the day, or were going to come later. Those that needed water at that time could get it in town.

Unusual? Yes, but not unplanned. Here was a woman who had charted her course specifically so she would not be seen. Later on we find out why. Here was a woman who had been married five times, and each time had ended with rejection. In this society women didn't have the right to divorce. The man she lived with now was only exploiting her, extending her neither his pledge or his name.

Imagine the stares she got from her community—those long, down-the-nose glances of people who would wince as if they had just smelled manure, and then would hurry away lest they would be somehow infected by her. She couldn't face it anymore, so she sneaked off to the farthest well at the hottest part of the day to be alone.

Even at a distance she would notice someone there, a stranger sitting by her well. I wonder if she thought about going back and trying again later. But she would look ridiculous, wouldn't she? She was halfway there with an empty pot on her head. She wasn't looking for relationship; she just wanted to be alone.

But it was not to be. She didn't speak to the stranger, whom she now recognized to be Jewish. She wanted to draw her water quickly and hurry away from the awkward moment before he said anything. But Jesus was ready for the ripened harvest. "Will you give me a drink?" he asked.

Her worst fear had come true. *At least he doesn't know me,* or so she might have thought. She didn't see him wince when he spoke to her. In fact, she winced first. "You are a Jew and I am a Samaritan." *If you don't know the real reason to despise me, shouldn't this be enough?*

But Jesus kept on, ignoring her plea to be left alone.

Let me note two important things that happened here. First, Jesus took the time to get to know a woman and her need. Where others saw a sinful woman, he saw someone thirsting for something she had not yet found. Without condoning her sin, he looked past it to the thirst that drove it, knowing number six wouldn't quench it. This was a woman who needed to drink from God's fountain.

Second, Jesus added some divine insight: "The fact is, you have had five husbands, and the man you now have is not your husband." He knew!

"He told me everything I ever did," is how she later reported the encounter to her friends. This man knew me and still extended to me an offer of life. Jesus showed her God's love, and she came to believe in him.

When the disciples got back with lunch, they were amazed that he was talking with a woman, much less a Samaritan. Did they wince in disdain at her? No matter, she was off to tell her family, "Could this be the Christ?"

Eventually her family and friends came to faith all because Jesus spent time with a woman who needed God's touch. No evangelistic rally downtown would have attracted her. She ran from crowds. This harvest needed a one-on-one encounter, which would also trigger so much more.

We often only see ministry in creating organizations and streamlined programs, not as a personal touch with rejected and hurting people. I don't want to indicate that such methods are wrong, but I do want us to take an objective look at how effective they are. What too often happens is that people with the most heart for ministry end up administrating programs instead of spending time with people. Programmed action easily replaces the power and love of God reaching out to touch others through changed lives.

We do not find the real ministry of the kingdom by finding a niche in a religious organization. We find it when we see God using us to touch other people. Of course there's a place for coordinated outreach, but I want to encourage those whose obedience doesn't fit such models. Don't be frustrated when other people's efforts receive notoriety that seems to escape you. Don't look for the applause of people. Look only for God's approval. Our ministry is far better measured by our faithfulness to him than by achieving the accolades of the religious sector of our society.

After his encounter with the woman at the well, the disciples tried to get Jesus to eat. But he replied, "I have food to eat that you know nothing about." There is something about being part of God's plan that is its own reward. "My food is to do the will of him who sent me and to finish his work."

Jesus affirms that we are not only branches on the vine, but also workers in the vineyard. Some sow, some reap, but all rejoice together as new lives are brought to Jesus. Don't exalt one above the other. The Corinthians did, and it produced a plethora of discord among them. Those who reap often benefit from others who have already done the harder work of sowing and nurturing.

Do you know what was the most major deterrent to the spread of the gospel? Not persecution. Not false teaching. Not the materialistic culture. Not the complacency of believers. It was jealousy.

Paul and Barnabas would go to a synagogue to proclaim that the Messiah had come. They always found receptive hearers. "Tell us more," they would plead, and invite them back next week. By the next week the place would be packed with people interested to hear what Paul and Barnabas would share. Those who had been around the synagogue for a long time found that offensive. Why should the crowds come now? Their jealousy caused them to reject what had stirred their hearts only a week before.

Jealousy is a powerful force. More than we would care to admit, it causes us to reject both the truth and those who incite our jealousy. There is too much jealousy and too much boasting in the body of Christ today over things only God has responsibility for. Resist it. Find your own obedience to God and pursue it whether or not it ever earns you any acclaim.

Fruitfulness for the vine comes in its season. The harvest may be ripe, but the harvesters may not be. As ready as the field was, Jesus sent his disciples back to Jerusalem to wait for the power that would come only from the Holy Spirit. The more God shapes you in his likeness, the more your opportunities will increase.

And don't limit your activities to the safely religious. Cultivate relationships with unbelievers so that they can taste God's character through you. Get involved in your community with nonbelievers at work, in your neighborhood, or through other activities God leads you to be part of. It doesn't have to be overtly Christian to be a place where God wants to make himself known through you.

Through these relationships God will show himself to the people around you. Let God choose how that happens. A vine does not harvest itself. Only the gardener does the harvesting.

Chapter 30

Just Whose Fruit Is It Anyway?

When the harvest time approached,
he sent his servants to the tenants to collect his fruit.
MATTHEW 21:34

Jesus told a story in which God planted a vineyard and entrusted its care to farmers. At harvest time he sent his servants to collect the fruit. You know the story: They preferred killing his servants, even the landowner's son, to sharing their fruit.

Their fruit. That's how they thought of it. "It's ours. We made it. We'll do with it what we want, and we don't want to share it."

Never mind that God had built the vineyard, planted each vine, and held the title to it all. He only assigned the care of the vineyard, not the ownership of its fruit. But the farmers failed to understand that fact. Instead of giving the landlord his due, they took possession of God's property and creation. It wasn't their fruit. It was God's fruit. He owned it and he made it.

Nothing will destroy the joy and bounty of the harvest faster (and turn God's blessing into our own source of destruction) than to misunderstand this foundational truth of the vineyard.

Israel missed it. God blessed them with great fruitfulness, but instead of offering it back to God in thanksgiving, they used it for their own desires. Hosea confronted them with their unfaithfulness:

Israel was a spreading vine; he brought forth fruit for himself. As his fruit increased, he built more altars; as his land prospered, he adorned his sacred stones. Their heart is deceitful, and now they must bear their guilt. The Lord will demolish their altars and destroy their sacred stones.

— HOSEA 10:1–2

The fruit belongs to God. Once we think that God's fruit is ours, any number of things can happen, and none of them are good. We use God's blessing for our own indulgence, or even to create our own gods and systems of worship.

But how we try to make the fruit ours! All too often when God blesses someone with gifts, ministry, influence, changed lives, or even material goods, they subtly begin to treasure the fruit of their lives above their relationship with God. It is far easier to seek God when our circumstances are desperate or when our lives are broken and despised. The gifts of God have always represented a greater threat to his people than did hardship.

The Israelites rarely forgot God when they were under attack or caught in famine. But in times of peace and tranquility they forgot him and turned to serve themselves either directly or through idols of their own creation. Their failure must be our lesson: God's blessing is not for our amusement; we are blessed to be a blessing to others.

Fruit grows to be given away. Hoarded fruit on the vine will only spoil and rot. If it's not picked and put to some other use, its blessing is lost. It is perhaps the saddest commentary on our generation that our view of Christianity is so tainted by self-interest.

To get people to worship, we must promise them the peace and tranquility it will bring to their heart. But worship by definition is self-abandonment. It is not singing in a service. Worship is offering our hearts to live in the Father's love . . . anything less twists worship into an exercise for our own amusement.

The same is true of ministry. If we can't hint to people that their service to God won't be richly rewarded in some material way, many are not interested.

In his kingdom, giving up your life is the key to living. No one demonstrated this better than the true vine himself. In living among us, Philippians tells us, Jesus emptied himself, not even regarding his equality with God as something he had to hold on to. He gave it up to become a servant to us.

Nothing marked his life better than his constant choices to give up his own temporal desires in order to obey his Father. He gave up fame and notoriety by refusing to use the power of God for his own advancement. He gave up his own safety by refusing to compromise truth in the face of religious leaders who wanted to contain him. He gave up his own personal comfort to bring God's kingdom throughout Israel. At the end of his life was the greatest giving up of all: He gave up his spirit to God.

In giving up he found the secret to being fruitful. He abandoned his own self-interest so that God the Father would be glorified: "I have brought you glory on earth by completing the work you gave me to do."

We grow in the kingdom of God, not by what we gain but by what we give away:

> *If anyone would come after me, he must deny himself and take up his cross and follow me. For whoever wants to save his life will lose it, but whoever loses his life for me will find it. What good will it be for a man if he gains the whole world, yet forfeits his soul? Or what can a man give in exchange for his soul?*
>
> — MATTHEW 16:24–26

The character shaped in our lives will be at God's disposal to use as he sees fit to nourish others or to multiply his vineyard. The promises he fulfills in us will be a light and encouragement to others. Even falling in love with one of God's fulfilled promises can be an idol that separates us from him.

Life in the church isn't measured by the power of a Sunday gathering or how well our programs work. It is measured by how effectively we release people to touch one another with the ministry of Jesus in firsthand contact with others. Increased size means that relationships give way to procedures, and spontaneity to planning. The only remedy is to let his work among us multiply instead of continuing to expand our most fruitful engagements into large institutions that need centralized bureaucracies to function.

Grapevines don't endlessly expand—they multiply into new grapevines that can continue to thrive in relative simplicity. How do we release even the connections we're enjoying to make relationships more accessible to others? Nothing challenges people more. Not only is change threatening, but tampering with relationships that have been key in God transforming people is sure to cause a stir.

We seek permanence where God seeks fruitfulness. We grasp for what we enjoy, not realizing that true joy comes by laying down our lives to see a greater grace fill our hearts. This transition may be difficult, but, in order to continue to be conduits of his life, it's a risk we must take. We have to be willing to lay down at every moment God's most precious blessings in a spirit of generosity that knows he can do again in our hearts what he has already done.

Letting God have the freedom to make those changes as he desires is what being a branch or a worker in his vineyard is all about. The fruit he has created in us was always intended to be a source of blessing for others. God sought to sow a spirit of generosity into the very fiber of his people. Even their physical crops were not to be harvested completely:

> *When you reap the harvest of your land, do not reap to the very edges of your field or gather the gleaning of your harvest. Do not go over your vineyard a second time or pick up the grapes that have fallen. Leave them for the poor and the alien. I am the Lord your God.*
>
> — LEVITICUS 19:9,10

God wants his people to be a generous people, never hoarding for themselves his blessings. When we realize that it all came from him anyway, it is easy for us to give it all back to him to use as he desires.

Chapter 31

What Happens When There Is No Harvest?

Though there are no grapes on the vines
and the yields produce no food yet will I rejoice in the Lord.
HABAKKUK 3:17,18

Can one embrace the promises of God in spring, endure the perils of summer, and still come through the harvest with no fruit to show for it?

It happened to my father in at least two seasons that I can remember. After nurturing the crop to completion, Dad still came up empty. The crop matured well enough, but the problem came at harvest. Because he makes raisins of his grapes, he picks them and lays them on the ground to dry on paper trays. This is when the raisin crop is most vulnerable. Should it rain heavily during those few days, the entire crop will rot right on the ground.

All the labor of a year is wiped out by a freak storm from the subtropics. It's rare for rain to find the San Joaquin Valley in September, and that's why he would lay them on the ground. But twice he paid for it rather severely. The crops were unsalvageable.

There are other dangers that can net the same result at harvest time. Insects or birds in large enough quantities can settle on a crop and devour it.

The enemies of fruitfulness don't just give up because fall has come. My father never thought his crop was safe until it was delivered to the packer. Then he could relax. Harvest was over.

Can this happen in the Father's vineyard? Can we faithfully pursue God only to have fruitfulness snatched away from us at the moment the promise emerges? I think not. But if I don't qualify that statement I'm afraid you'll misunderstand it, and with it, God as well.

The reason I would say no is because Isaiah's words are so clear:

> *As the rain and the snow come down from heaven,*
> *and do not return to it without watering the earth and*
> *making it bud and flourish, so that it yields seed for the*
> *sower and bread for the eater, so is my word that goes*
> *out from my mouth: It will not return to me empty, but*
> *will accomplish what I desire and achieve the purpose*
> *for which I sent it.*
>
> — ISAIAH 55:10,11

As long as we continue to remain in a growing relationship of trust with Jesus, that relationship cannot help but bear fruit in our lives. However, many carry unrealistic expectations of what that fruitfulness may mean. They confuse being fruitful with being successful in the world's eyes, or living in comfortable bliss. They couldn't be more wrong.

Take Stephen, for instance, who was brutally murdered for his faith. He was the first non-apostle to emerge in the early church with a compelling understanding of the new covenant. Just as he was coming into his own, perhaps after his first and what proved to be his last sermon, he was stoned. Was Stephen a harvest aborted? It may look like that to some, but his death proved to bring a greater glory to God's work in the world. His life bore fruit, and it still does through the testimony of Scripture.

The litany of Paul's struggles on behalf of the gospel was legendary as listed in 2 Corinthians 11:24–27:

🐾 Five times I received from the Jews the forty lashes minus one.

🐾 Three times I was beaten with rods.

- Once I was stoned.
- Three times I was shipwrecked.
- I spent a night and a day in the open sea.
- I have been constantly on the move.
- I have been in danger from rivers, in danger from bandits, in danger from my own countrymen, in danger from Gentiles, in danger in the city, in danger in the country, in danger at sea, and in danger from false brothers.
- I have labored and toiled and have often gone without sleep.
- I have known hunger and thirst and have often gone without food.
- I have been cold and naked.

Does this sound like a man loved of God? If not, then perhaps your perception of God's love is skewed. God loved Paul just as much as he loves you, but that must not translate to the false expectation that God's love will insulate us from all pain and discomfort in this age. Rather, his love will carry us through to the fullness of his glory and to an even greater harvest.

Even as Paul sat in a prison cell in Rome, abandoned and lonely, his execution just around the corner, his heart was steadfast in the Lord's victory. He didn't doubt his own fruitfulness even though many of the churches in Asia had abandoned him.

> *I have fought the good fight, I have finished the race,*
> *I have kept the faith. Now there is in store for me the*
> *crown of righteousness, which the Lord, the righteous*
> *Judge, will award to me on that day.* — 2 TIMOTHY 4:7,8

Don't look to your circumstances for the measure of your harvest. You simply cannot trust your perceptions of them. The only way harvest is aborted in the life of a believer is if we give in to the enemy's devices to abandon our faith in the midst of difficult times.

Whether the enemy thwarted my dad's harvest, or whether he was simply a victim of capricious weather, what was really at stake was his faith. Here's where I learned more about faith than any other single experience.

Many times I had seen rain clouds threaten and had prayed earnestly that God would protect our crop. I remember times when the rain pummeled our neighbors' vineyard but stopped almost directly along our property line. How we rejoiced that God's hand had spared us!

The first time God didn't stop the rains, I watched my dad carefully. I saw him one afternoon staring out at his field, the rain pelting down in sheets. An inch had already fallen on the drying grapes a few days before and had damaged them severely. This second storm would spell their end. He knew that. I saw the helplessness and disappointment in his eyes and I felt as bad for him in that moment as I've ever felt for anyone. Didn't God care? How could he let this happen?

"What are we going to do, Dad?" I asked, wondering how we would eat the next year.

Through his disappointment, his response was clear: "The Lord is faithful." After a long pause, "We'll just have to see how the Lord will provide for us in the year ahead."

And provide he did.

I didn't miss any meals that year, and more importantly, I learned a valuable lesson. Confidence placed in a completed crop or a hefty bank account is a vain hope. Hope is better placed in God, who has more options to fulfill his will than we could ever guess.

Even the most difficult trials can enhance our faith, and therefore our spiritual fruitfulness. That's why the prophet Habakkuk could exclaim:

> *Though the fig tree does not bud*
> *and there are no grapes on the vines,*
> *though the olive crop fails*
> *and the fields produce no food . . .*
> *yet will I rejoice in the Lord,*
> *I will be joyful in God my Savior.*
> *The sovereign Lord is my strength.*
>
> — HABAKKUK 3:17-19

Chapter 32

The Growing Is Not Yet Over

Let us live up to what we have already attained.
PHILIPPIANS 3:16

In the euphoria of harvest it is easy to reap the fruit of our past diligence and lose sight of its continuing necessity. It is easy to enjoy God's abundance and start to overlook our continued need to foster an ongoing connection to the vine.

Scientists tell us that in the final stages of ripening, all the strength of the vine is drawn into the grapes. The storehouses in the trunk and roots are depleted. After the grapes are harvested, however, the storehouses are replenished to prepare the vine for another growing season. This growth continues until the beginning days of winter, when the leaves finally wither and fall to the ground.

The cycle of sowing and reaping continues. Next year's crop has already formed in the buds of the first-year canes now on the vine. The size of each bunch and the size of the entire crop has already been determined by the health of the vine during the last year.

The nutrients stored now will not be needed in the approaching winter because the vine will go dormant. But they will be there next spring when the branch explodes with new life. They will live off what it stores now before those leaves are strong enough to produce their own nutrition.

"Remain in me." There is no season that the branch cannot afford to heed that glorious invitation. In the glory of harvest it is easy to grow complacent and forget about the God who has accomplished all these things in us. Like the Israelites in the Old Testament, it is easy to cry out to God in pain and conflict, knowing how much we need him. But whenever God delivered them and brought them into a place of abundance, they would forget about him and either turn to idols or simply give in to an indulgent lifestyle.

I've seen it happen so often with people. They cry out to God during a time of crisis and begin to discover what it means to live in him. As that begins to bear some significant fruit in their lives they either begin to take him for granted or, worse yet, they begin to think that it is their own strength or ingenuity that produced the fruit. Initially God gets pushed to the background and then as the relationship withers, he may continue to get lip service from them but not the focus that allows the relationship to keep growing.

Grapes are not a one-season crop. They produce crop after crop, year after year. The cycle of growth continues in our hearts as well, and as with all living things we are either growing or withering. Many a believer has made the mistake of assuming that just because God is doing good things in their life, that alone will be sufficient to sustain their relationship with him. How many of us have seen men and women move in some incredible gifts, only to watch them suddenly take a great fall. The vineyard teaches us that such falls are not sudden at all. They result from days of not remaining in the vine and drawing on its life.

When our own relationship with the vine gets compromised, no matter how great the harvest we're in the midst of, we have begun to wither. An inner emptiness even in harvest can tell us that we've lost connection with the vine.

At all costs, cling to your friendship with Jesus as more valuable than anything in this life. Cherish his presence and linger there often to replenish your life in him. "Draw near," the writer of Hebrews said. By doing so we allow our life in him to deepen. Listen to his voice and let him show you what he is doing in you beyond the harvest itself.

God wants to bring you through to another season, and still another beyond that, until the day when the final harvest comes and his reapers bring history to an end. This is the harvest for which we all yearn with passions that will never be fulfilled in this age. We were not created for the sinful, finiteness of this broken world. We were created for all eternity in purity with Christ forever. All of your dreams and hopes will not be fulfilled here.

Even those in the great roll call of faith in Hebrews 11 didn't receive the fullness of what was promised them in this life.

> *These were all commended for their faith, yet none of them received what had been promised. God had planned something better for us so that only together with us would they be made perfect.*
>
> —HEBREWS 11:39,40

All of God's working in us does not have its fulfillment here. He is preparing us for a greater day. God is preparing us for all eternity in his presence. What we've valued most dear in this life of eternal consequence is being saved for us there.

For now, however, the harvest is past, the storehouses are fully replenished. Winter is just around the corner. You can already feel the chill in the air.

Winter
Resting and Restaging

This is what the Sovereign LORD,
the Holy One of Israel, says:
"In repentance and rest is your salvation,
in quietness and trust is your strength . . ."
ISAIAH 30:15

The glory of harvest is past. As winter sets in, the vine looks like it's withering as the leaves turn brown against the dull, gray sky. Eventually they drop to the ground, leaving the vine barren. But it would be wrong to assume the vine is dead, even though it appears so. It has only grown dormant. The branches are resting in the silence of winter and during this time the Master of the vineyard does his best work to prepare it for a new cycle of fruitfulness.

Chapter 33

Days of Rest and Preparation

Come to me, all you who are weary and burdened,
and I will give you rest.
Take my yoke upon you and learn from me . . .
and you will find rest for your souls.
MATTHEW 11:28-29

As winter encroaches, the joy of the harvest becomes a fading memory. The leaves begin to turn yellow, having finished their work for the year. The vineyard is beginning its season of rest to prepare for next year's harvest.

Winter finally comes at the first nighttime freeze, which in this valley is usually in the waning days of November. Rest comes quickly as the leaves turn a dirty brown, wilted reminders of a rich heritage, and then fall earthward.

The vineyard lies in chaos. Debris fills the rows between the vines. The canes, no longer hidden by their leafy dress, twist and turn inside each other in vivid disarray. Dark bunches of rotted grapes missed in the harvest hang limply, uncovered by winter's nakedness. The wounds of the growing season are obvious. Some canes have broken off, while others were split open by the weight of the ripening grapes. They have even pulled down the wire between the vines, where it now slumps from grapestake to grapestake.

This chaos of early winter stands in marked contrast to how the vines will look at its end. Only a few months from now these vines will stand pruned and neatly tied to a restretched wire. The debris below will be worked into the soil, compost for the next harvest.

Winter is where the growth cycle begins. I have waited to the end to describe it because only in the aftermath of fruitfulness can we understand its value. It may seem harsh for the vine, but it is not. The vine must rest if the farmer is going to restage it for the year to come.

We have winters in our growth cycles too. Spiritual winter comes when the external fruitfulness of our life begins to fade, and God rests and prepares us for another crop.

Often our circumstances will signal the coming of winter, just as in the vineyard. They seem to turn against us. We are doing all the same things, but nothing is as fruitful as it was before. You may ask yourself, "Why is everything drying up?" Fear might even set in as you wonder if you will ever be fruitful again.

We've all been through moments like that. Instead of recognizing the onset of a new season, we usually redouble our efforts to try to keep winter's effects at bay. We pretend that it is still fall and try harder to produce fruit by our own efforts.

But winter is not a time for our greater efforts; it's time for the branches to enter into their rest. In these moments, as the distractions diminish, we are drawn into a deeper connection with the vine and find our fellowship with him far greater than in any other season.

This is where we learn to rest in him. He is doing a work without our help except for our surrender to his purpose. If we learn to rest in him in winter, it won't be long until spring sweeps across our spirits again and fruitfulness once again graces our branches.

Chapter 34

Fading Glory

Forgetting what is behind and straining toward what is ahead,
I press on toward the goal to win the prize
for which God has called me heavenward in Christ Jesus.
PHILIPPIANS 3:13–14

It's not easy to watch God's glory fade at season's end, and even harder not to do anything to stop it.

The blossoms of spring needed to wither and fall so that the fruit could form. In the fall the ripened fruit had to surrender to the farmer as his abundant crop. Now the branch must yield again, but this time it is a far greater yielding. For now it is not just blossoms and fruit that need to surrender to the creeping coldness of winter, but also the glory of the branch itself.

To be a fruitful branch on Jesus' vine it seems that you really have to do only two things: one, remain in the vine, treasuring friendship with Jesus every day, and two, let go of everything else, even the success of the harvest. *Never grasp anything too tightly.* Real followers of Jesus learn the secret of letting go. God moves on and invites us to go with him. Our greatest danger lies in trying to cling to past joys and glories missing out on what is yet to come.

The glory of the branches cannot be found in its blooms, its fruit, or even its leaves and canes. Its glory exists only in the continuing relationship it holds with the vine. That never changes.

From season to season the one constant source of fulfillment is our friendship with Jesus, and every good thing he brings into our lives will test whether it is him we love, or the things he has given us.

It is easier for us to fall in love with the trappings of our faith than to keep our love for Jesus aflame. Almost without noticing, we substitute those trappings for the relationship itself. We find ourselves passionate for forms of worship or ministry more than we are for him. It is a subtle trap, and anyone who doesn't admit to becoming its victim at one point or another is either not telling it straight or not thinking it straight.

As believers realize that our security or glory is not in anything external, or even in anything that God has done. Unless we continually forget the things that lie behind us and keep pressing toward the real prize we'll find ourselves sitting stagnant in the decay of past glory. When Paul talks about forgetting what lies behind, it wasn't just failures and sins he was referring to, but even more importantly, successes and joys as well.

Never is danger greater for a believer than at the onset of spiritual winter. As we've seen, the harvest is a time of euphoria. Almost daily, opportunities to touch people with God's power fill our lives, and we watch God do amazing things through us. In such times righteousness seems to flow from us like a raging river. Even our most difficult moments are swallowed up by this overreaching joy.

But like all seasons, harvest runs its course.

It's easy to panic if we don't appreciate how God works in various seasons. *What's happened? Why is my joy slipping away? Why am I not as effective as I used to be?*

Our first conclusion is that something is wrong with us. We know the frailties of our flesh, and they provide a ready source for personal blame. But in doing so we forget that God's work through us comes only by his grace. We didn't earn it the first time and we certainly don't now. We try repentance, but it doesn't seem to be the answer. While it might refresh our walk with the Lord, we still watch helplessly as the harvest continues to wither.

Most of us prefer to hide the fading. *If I don't let anybody see it, they won't know that the harvest is over.* So we cover it up, most commonly with busyness. With our own effort, we push through what used to seem so graced before.

The onset of winter is not something to be lamented. These are the days where the vineyard is restored for a new year. The pace slows, and I've never met a farmer who wasn't relieved to have the crop in as winter approached. This is not embarrassment; it is nature's way, which is to say, quite accurately, that it is also God's way.

Any act of ministry in the kingdom of God is not open-ended, continuing until his second coming. God harvests in specific seasons and through specific people. If we recognize this fact we can allow harvest times to come to completion, and then celebrate them and let go.

God does a work, mines it for its maximum usefulness, and then lets it go to raise up other opportunities. How many people are trapped administering programs that have long since been lifeless? Can't we find the courage to say that something can be finished without it being a failure?

We can't live in harvest all of the time, at least not without destroying the life of the branch. Those who define normal Christianity as the days of harvest will be frustrated most of their lives. Such times will come to an end, not by your failures, but by God's design.

A new season is at hand, and that is not a failure unless your priorities are skewed. If you look for fruit in the middle of winter, you will be a failure by definition. But if you are continuing to pursue your friendship with Jesus, you'll find it is just another season to enjoy him regardless of what's going on around you.

Unlike Moses, whose glory faded away, Paul said that we embrace a covenant whose glory only increases. But don't judge that by externals. The true glory is the depth of friendship, which Christ builds in our lives, and the shaping that makes us more like him. That process passes through a variety of seasons, some more glorious than others externally, but all of them inviting us to greater touches of his grace.

Winter is a glorious time when God reshapes us from the effects of our past activities in order to release us to more fruitful days ahead. In doing so he tests the affections of our hearts. Have we done what we've done because of our love and obedience to Christ, or has it been for our own sense of fulfillment and success? The onset of winter will let you know for sure.

If you have a hard time letting go because you need your busyness to feel important, then perhaps the reshaping is more needed than you know. I used to feel threatened whenever my life seemed to slow down, concerned that I was losing my edge or that God was no longer blessing me. Instead of letting God deal with those insecurities, I looked for other ways to busy myself . . . you know, I would join another committee, plan another outreach, or start another Bible study. I didn't like the quiet. I wanted to be fruitful for God, and in doing so I resisted his work when he was slowing my life. By burying myself in busyness, I tried to run from the rest I so desperately needed.

I think it showed that I was more in love with what I called ministry than I was in love with him. But God was patient with my misdirected zeal. He even blessed some of those outreaches and Bible studies in ways that still amaze me. But I have since learned that when things slow down, God is addressing something inside of me. He's moving me to a new place of dependence.

While our trust is developed in the heat of summer, it is most needed in the winter. Here we discover whether our life and joy are truly in him, or whether or not we have begun to find our identity in the things we have done or the success of our plans. We will never hold our past loosely if we don't know that our future is secure in God's hands.

The priority that takes center stage in winter is that vital link between the vine and branch. If you have the courage to set aside the ministries that God has brought to completion in your life, to look away from past successes, you can take advantage of the opportunity to let him deepen your friendship with him. As things grow quiet, you'll see more clearly God's direction in your life, and even some of your own less-than-pure motives that snuck in or were exposed by the growing season. Don't fear it or resist it. It only provides the opportunity for the Father to do an even deeper work in you in the winter ahead.

Chapter 35

The Colder the Better

Be still, and know that I am God.
PSALM 46:10

What is more serene than the earth under a blanket of freshly fallen snow? We may appreciate such a scene best when looking out on it from the comfy confines of a winter cabin with a roaring fire in the hearth. The morning after a snowstorm is an awesome sight. The vivid blue sky almost pours down through the trees and the sun reflects its splendor off the white blanket below.

But to really experience its beauty, you must go out *in* it. That's when you notice the stillness. Nature has come to a standstill. The only sound to be heard is snow crunching underfoot.

Take that same image into the vineyard. Our valley is not normally snow-covered. It snowed once on our vineyard, and only four inches at that. However, our winters are filled with a low, gray overcast that swaddles the vineyard into the same serenity of the most ideal snowy winter landscape.

The heat of summer sought to destroy the vine's fruitfulness, but persevering through it was necessary to ripen the fruit. Winter is also a hostile climate, except that this time we don't prevail by perseverance but by patience and rest.

Few of us look on winter with great longing to be refreshed and rested. Instead we dread the harsh climate and endure it by looking forward to the warmer days of summer. But it is just the opposite for a vine. Summer was the season of warfare as it battled the hostile forces bent on destroying the fruit. Fall, too, was a time of multiplied activity and intensive effort. The cold of winter lulls the vine to a much-needed rest. It is during this season of rest and restaging that God invites us ever closer to him.

There are two ways that God brings our spiritual journeys into a winter season. One is circumstantial—when the activities and opportunities we've been involved in slow down appreciably. The second is by invitation, where God asks us to lay some of our things aside and for a time to give greater attention to our relationship with him. Both signal an end to one season of fruitfulness in order to prepare us for another.

There are many instances of such seasons in Scripture, though given their nature we don't always get a great deal of detail with them. Moses, on the backside of the desert, was in a time of transition, from a prince in Pharaoh's court to an ambassador and deliverer on God's behalf. The children of Israel passing through the wilderness also comprised a winter season as God sought to forge a people who could go into the Promised Land and be fruitful. Jesus' experience in the wilderness after his baptism also provided God an opportunity to prepare him for his public days of ministry.

Because of these examples the winter season is often referred to as a wilderness experience. If by wilderness we mean a time where God calls us to a season of undistracted attention away from the busyness that ensnares us, I will wholeheartedly agree with the term.

But I've heard many people define the wilderness as a time when God withdraws his conscious presence from us in order to deepen our faith. Nowhere does Scripture suggest such an idea. God wants to increase our dependence upon him, not teach us how to live without him. I will grant you that God will allow certain methods we've used to touch him to dry up, but only so that we'll come looking for him in fresh ways. In fact, many of our winters begin just that way: The old patterns grow lifeless, and God beckons us to fresh discovery.

The vine does not come to winter worn out by the harvest. In fact, it has more strength reserves at the end of fall than at any other time of the year. A healthy vine rests while a starved vine withers, and the distinction between these two, though not always evident in winter, will be obvious next spring.

Being burned out is not a normal period of any growth cycle. Admittedly, recognition of burn-out is not easy—burned-out people always look their best the day before they crash. They are so willing and helpful that they usually serve as the model zealous believer. But if you listen closely you'll see their weariness, hear their complaints that others aren't doing enough, or find a family at home crying out for their attention.

Rather than being applauded, these people could be lovingly challenged. Burnout results from activity that doesn't flow out of an intimacy with him, but rather out of our personal insecurities. This is so people will think well of us, or because we think we can earn God's approval by our hard work. Real healing cannot come by just "getting away from it all" for a time and then plunging back into your activities again. Until your security is grounded in a growing relationship with the vine, you will continue to try to hide your emptiness in an exhausting regimen of religious activity.

God will still take a burned-out believer into winter to prune away his dependence on self-effort, but it only works if he recognizes the problem. Only as we draw near to him and recognize and depend on his work again, can we truly understand what he is asking of us. True fruitfulness flows out of our growing trust in his work and not from when we feel obligated to the expectations of others.

Those in ministry are especially at risk of finding their identity in their achievements rather than in their relationship to Christ. Many won't discover it until they are shipwrecked on the weariness of their own hyperactivity. And too many resist God's call to find their peace in him, and not in what they perceive to be the size and scope of their ministry.

When you recognize the onset of winter in your spiritual life, give in to God's call to stillness. Find extra time to seek his face, and be patient when it may not come with ease. It's not that God can't speak to us in our busyness, it's just that the noise of our own self-generated activity drowns him out. Of course this doesn't mean that we should abandon all our responsibilities and go sit in the desert. But it does mean that we can rest from our labors and stop striving so hard for human success in order that we may see him and follow him with greater freedom in our hearts.

Winter is God drawing us to the quiet, where he does his deepest work. I've never heard it scientifically explained, but every farmer knows that the colder the winter is, the better the crop will be in the season to come. Mild winters lead to average yields. It seems the farther the sap is driven into the vine, the more explosive its return will be come spring.

Chapter 36

The Pause That Refreshes

He makes me lie down in green pastures,
he leads me beside quiet waters.
PSALM 23:2

I've seen worn-out grape branches—either from overuse or because insects have eaten out the inside. These are not easy to see under the profuse canopy of leaves that hide the branches much of the year, but once the leaves have fallen off they are easy to spot. Most of the branch is no longer connected to the vine; it holds on only by the slimmest connection.

Once a branch has overspent itself, it is worthless. The canes that spring from it are weak and lifeless, and most of them could never reach the wire to be used again for another year. Many of these are cut off with a saw to allow a new branch to grow from that side of the vine.

Fortunately, God doesn't deal so severely with worn-out believers, or we would be in real trouble. Yet, I have no doubt that he laments them just as much as the farmer does a broken branch. "Harassed and helpless, like sheep without a shepherd," is how Jesus described a crowd of people. You can always tell a shepherd-less sheep just like you can tell a gardener-less vineyard—they are weary and worn-out, surviving, coping, and all the while slowly dying.

The slowed days of winter fly in the face of our frenetic pace of life. This is the gardener leading his vineyards to rest in the same way the shepherd takes his sheep to green pastures and quiet waters. There they lie down to rest. The waters that nurse them are quiet, not raging.

If we learned this well enough, perhaps the expression "to be busy for God" would be an oxymoron. It is the world that invites us to busyness. Take it from one who used to find most of his identity in a crammed schedule, proving by activity his worth to God. It is a fool's trap that has made busyness a coveted merit badge in the kingdom of God.

God doesn't want our busyness; he wants our trust. Having our trust, he knows we will respond to him and his ways as life unfolds before us.

But how can we trust him if we're not still enough to hear his voice? We have let our lives become so complicated that we are always exhausted. Running on increasing doses of adrenaline, we miss the voice that comes only in the stillness. That's not to say there won't be periods when activities and challenges may press us from every side, but we just shouldn't pitch our tent there. God will lead us through those places and then back out again to lie down in those green pastures.

Winter depicts the vineyard at rest. During these months two important things will happen. The first is that the rest will refresh the vines. It's time for a break. The second is that the vines are pruned to make them more fruitful. The two go together. Only out of rest and quiet can we let the Lord shape our lives, for that is the source of our strength.

> *In repentance and rest is your salvation, in quietness and trust is your strength, but you would have none of it.* — ISAIAH 30:15

Why then do we resist him in our attempts to compress as much activity as possible into virtually every moment of the day? Even most of my recreational pursuits have another agenda in mind and many worry in their idle moments that they aren't doing enough for their family, church, or themselves.

The fact that we avoid moments of quiet may tell us just how spiritually bankrupt we are. At every point our senses take in a wide array of sights and sounds. Even in times of prayer and contemplation it is a challenge simply to wade through the clutter that fills our minds to find that place of quiet.

Winter is an amazing opportunity to remember that it is in the stillness that we come to know him. And furthermore, it is in that rest that he invites us into the process that makes us truly fruitful for him.

Chapter 37

Submitting to the Master's Pruning

He cuts off every branch in me that bears no fruit,
while every branch that does bear fruit he prunes so that
it will be even more fruitful.

JOHN 15:2

The sap slows to nearly a standstill. It is now the middle of winter. The dried leaves have all fallen, and only the canes remain. Now the winter labor of the farmer can begin. There's one major activity that the farmer attends to in the winter, and according to John 15, it is the most significant one. There is no action the farmer will take in a year that will have more impact on the health and fruitfulness of the vine than pruning.

Most of the time the farmer cares for the vine by protecting it from enemies who want to destroy it. But pruning gives him the opportunity to shape the vine to make it as fruitful as possible. That's why my father hated to hire any outsiders to do this particular job. Hasty and careless pruning by those who only wanted to get the job done quickly could ruin the vine for seasons to come.

So on cold winter mornings during our Christmas school break and on weekends my father would take his four sons into the vineyard to prune. Bundled up against the cold, we could barely move, but with pruning shears in hand we would follow.

A vine in winter is a confusing array of light tan canes that sprawl from a branch like broken watch springs. All emerged the previous spring as flexible green vines, but they have now become woody sticks that shoot from every corner of the vine. Small dark-brown buds are spaced several inches apart down the entire length of every cane, some stretching to twelve feet or more in length. The buds are about half the size of a pencil eraser and quite hard. In each bud bunches of fruit for the coming year are already formed. During the summer, while the current crop was ripening, the next year's was also developing.

That next crop is all right here even in the middle of winter. Each bud contains one primary bunch, fully formed, albeit microscopic. In each bud there are also one or two secondary bunches that will sprout if something happens to damage the first. The only problem is that there are too many bunches for the vine to carry to harvest. Each cane holds twenty to twenty-five buds, and there are anywhere from forty to sixty canes on each vine. There are far more buds on the vine than it could ever possibly sustain.

Unpruned grapevines will grow into the next season. In fact, in one way they'll look healthier than a pruned vine. Foliage will burst forth everywhere, and so will the small grape bunches. But most will fall off, and those that don't will stay small and not ripen fully. The vine will be overwhelmed, and in the next season there will be no grapes at all. No new bunches will be formed in the buds that summer because the vine is overextended. That's why pruning is so essential to vine growth.

Snip. Snip. Snip. The shears tear into the vine, reducing the number of canes to *only five*! That's all the vine will be able to support in the coming year. The rest are cut off and dragged to the middle of the row, where they will be chewed up as compost. What remains is a vine radically transformed from confusion and chaos into a simple, stately form with five canes arching gracefully into the winter sky.

From our vantage point we might think most of the potential fruitfulness of the vine was cut off. But fruitfulness is an intentional process and it does not arise when our natural inclinations run riot.

We cannot do all things well and we cannot be busy all of the time. If we don't focus on getting a few things done right, we'll find ourselves spread increasingly thin and decreasingly fruitful in the things God cares about.

That's why the Master of the vineyard prunes, and that process is not without its discomfort. Where all the canes are cut off, open wounds remain. They will heal soon enough, but we now see why pruning can only be safely done in the dormancy of winter. Only after the sap has slowed and the vine is at rest will pruning do the least amount of damage. Damage? Yes, pruning is organized destruction.

Even the Greek word used for pruning in John 15 conveys that meaning. Everywhere else in the New Testament it is translated as *destroy* or *demolish*. John 15 is its only positive use, but it does show the objective of the pruning. The number of canes that the vine needed last year to provide foliage for last year's crop to ripen is now a threat to the vine in the year ahead.

It is surgery of the highest order, and unless the branch is at rest when the process begins, this cutting would destroy the branch itself. During winter the sap does not flow (or else it would drain the vine's strength), and diseases and pests that would infect the wounds are also dormant. In an environment where we are being refreshed by his presence, the wounds are not so painful or so likely to be used by the enemy to engender bitterness or rebellion in our lives. In the climate of quiet and peace he can prune us with minimal damage and maximum effectiveness.

Pruned correctly, the vine's growth will be spread out evenly over the vine; it will carry the right amount of fruit that it can take to term, and its shape will facilitate the other aspects of care that the farmer will give the vine over the coming growing season.

What a marvelous picture of the surgery that God has to do periodically in our lives! He prunes us so that we bear even more fruit. This means he cuts away things that clutter our lives. Yes, he wounds us, but these are the wounds of a friend, who cuts softly and tenderly, realizing that separation is painful and will cause hurt.

A part of pruning is for God to cut away where worldly passions and distractions siphon off our spiritual life. Attitudes surface that we either had not recognized before or had disguised by our rationalizations. During pruning we will have a keener sense of our weaknesses because God is calling us to repentance and cutting ties where the enemy keeps a foothold. Sin, if we refuse to let God cut it away, will eventually catch up with us and lead us astray.

He also cuts to restage our lives under his purpose. Growth and harvest have a way of multiplying opportunities in our lives, but those opportunities have the capacity not only to spread our lives so thin that we are fruitless, but also to distract us from our friendship with Jesus. If you want to stay busy even as God leads you to winter, you will have plenty of opportunities, but take them at your own peril.

Pruning is God's invitation to lay down those things that no longer need to take up our time and energy and move on to new things that will inspire us and help others. Through it, God resets our focus so that we can concentrate on what he wants us to do. Better to do one thing fruitfully than a lot of things that only turn out to be empty foliage.

I know people like that. In fact, I've been like that myself. Externally I looked productive, busily rushing from one meeting to another or jumping from one project to the next. Leaves everywhere! How intoxicating busyness can be. But I couldn't find the fruit. My spiritual life was so diluted by my myriad of activities that none of them were bearing anything more than paltry, unripened fruit.

Busyness is not the goal of a conscientious believer; fruitfulness is. Not every request that comes my way is God's will for me to accept. Good opportunities are not necessarily godly ones. Expectations pushed on us by others are not the directions Jesus invites us to follow.

Paul wrote to Titus that, "The grace of God teaches us to say no." That means we can say no to the worldly passions that destroy us and no to the opportunities that overwhelm us.

Notice that it's not fear that teaches us to say no, but grace. Because we can trust God and know that he will lead us into the fullness of joy, we are free to say no even to the things that we desire, whether good or bad.

Jesus said no to the enemy's temptations, knowing that God's way was better. He didn't rush to Lazarus' side when he first heard he was sick. He stayed two days longer to finish what he was doing before he joined the friends he deeply loved. Given Paul's explanations in his epistles, he didn't rush to churches that desired him to come either. He followed God's agenda instead.

Recognizing that we are branches on his vine will free us to focus on the few things that God has *really* called us to do. That's the only way to be fruitful. Draw near to God and let him show you what his plans are. His grace will teach you to say no to those that aren't.

But say no you must, for unlike the grapevines I approached with my pruning shears that had absolutely no say in the matter, it seems that we actually do. God's pruning requires our submission. We have to willingly let go of that which he wants to prune from us, and even after he prunes it, he won't prevent us from grabbing it back. He will only continue to gently call us to lay it down.

The life that listens to God is not a whirlwind of activity, it is rather a focused life. It results in simplicity, power, and joy. Don't resist God's pruning. It is your fulfillment and fruitfulness he is working to enhance.

Chapter 38

Die to It

Then Jesus said to his disciples, "If anyone would come after me,
he must deny himself and take up his cross and follow me.
For whoever wants to save his life will lose it,
but whoever loses his life for me will find it."
MATTHEW 16:24–25

A youth outreach to three villages in central Mexico offered a prime opportunity to learn the depths of love. Dan, one of the leaders of the outreach, came back with an amazing story that carries an amazing lesson.

Everything does not always run smoothly on such trips, and it's easy for people to get on each other's nerves. Every time the actions of others frustrated Dan, God saw to it that a missionary they worked with in the area was nearby. Seeing Dan's frustration begin to build, he would quietly sneak behind Dan and whisper in his ear, "Dan, die to it!" That was all, nothing more. But a gentle smile would sneak past Dan's lips as he would give in to the vital message it held.

Not all wars need to be fought, not all preferences have to be championed, and not all hurts need to be ironed out. Some things we can just die to, giving up what we are seeking in order to yield to the greater purpose God puts before us. If "dying to it," sounds like a painful means to earn God's blessing in your life, you're missing the point. Dan's testimony was like a splash of cool water on a hot face. For him, dying to it meant living for something greater than his own temporal satisfaction.

Laying down your life in the reality of God's love is not an onerous demand; it is a joyful freedom. You don't have to vent every frustration. You don't have to get your way in every circumstance. Sometimes you can just die to the drive to put yourself first and trust the Father's hand above your own schemes.

Whether it is yielding up the blossoms of spring, dying to our vain self-preferences in the onslaught of summer, yielding our fruit in the fall, or giving up some fruitful endeavor to God's pruning in winter, the vine seems to constantly give up *what was* in order to participate in *what's next*. Holding on to something in the past is a certain way to choke off your life in the vine and miss what he wants to give you today.

No doubt that is hardest where the joys are the greatest, but unless we learn to lay down our lives when he asks it of us and die to our own ambitions and desires, we miss the wonder of his resurrection life. While Jesus most demonstrated that reality when he gave his physical life for us in the horrors of the cross, that wasn't the only place he gave up his life for others around him. It was the way he lived.

Most of the farmer's efforts in the vineyard are not spectacular. They are often dirty, menial tasks done in the harshest conditions— the blazing heat of summer or the biting cold of winter. Some might consider vineyard work demeaning, similar to how the disciples felt about a different task a few hours before . . .

They had come to the upper room with feet soiled from the dusty roads of the city. Since their room was borrowed, there was no designated host to attend to the needs of the guests.

How awkward those first moments in the room must have been—lots of dirty feet and no one to wash them. They must have thought about it, certain that someone else was supposed to do it. Let Judas, he paid for the room. What about Bartholomew? He was the last one chosen, wasn't he? They ultimately decided to skip it altogether because dinner was ready and no one had volunteered to serve the others.

That is, until Jesus tied a towel around his waist. Though some obviously didn't want him to do it, no one else offered. Graciously he washed their feet. Some have suggested that Jesus did so to teach them humility. It appears John would disagree. He said Jesus washed their feet expressly to show them the "full extent of his love." (John 13:1) This was not a show. It was a photograph of love in its most complete form. Jesus cared about them enough to do the most menial task they had not even considered doing for him.

Greater love has no one than this, that he lay down his life for his friends. Jesus told them his friendship was not borne out of convenience but steeped in affection so deep it thought nothing of sacrificing for the simple blessing of another. This is the affection that ties the branches to the vine—a friendship so enduring that one would easily give for the need of another. Simply, friends lay down their lives for each other.

Jesus was that kind of friend. He would prove it again in a few hours on the cross, but in this moment he showed them the full extent of his love when he didn't consider it beneath his dignity to wash their dirty feet—for Judas as much as for Peter.

But there is a larger lesson here. The love Jesus demonstrated is the love he asked from the disciples. I want you to lay down your lives for me as well. How? By dying on a cross?

No, he had something else in mind. Even though most of the disciples in that circle would eventually die for him, their death was not the sacrifice he sought. "Love each other as I have loved you." He called them to lay down their lives for him by laying it down for each other. Perhaps this is the harder of the two. Sometimes it is easier to die for someone than to live alongside them.

Except for the call to remain in him, this is the only other lesson of the vineyard that Jesus repeated. He told them they could remain in him if they obeyed his commands, and then specified that his command was that they love each other. This is the one obedience where all others find their meaning. It is the fulfillment of every law.

This was not an abstract call to love all of God's people. There were only twelve people in that vineyard on the evening Jesus told his tale. I wonder if Jesus even gestured around the circle as he spoke the words. The love he asked of them couldn't be hidden in generalities. These men knew one another, weaknesses and all. "Surely he doesn't mean the power-grabbing Zebedee boys. Or Peter, the man who would be leader except that he can't get his foot out of his mouth long enough to be of much use. Certainly he doesn't mean Thomas whose incessant questioning drives me crazy." Yes. That's exactly who he meant.

Love. It is the simplest reality of the vineyard. Living in his love will free us to live open handed and open hearted, not having to grasp past glories or hog the limelight. Knowing his affection for us, we are free to respond to his working in those seasons where we must let go even of those things most meaningful to us in order to be part of the unfolding journey.

And having been loved, the most natural response is to share that love with others as freely as it was given to us. Here is purpose, fulfillment, and fruitfulness coming together in our lives. Learning to live loved and loving others fulfills every desire that Father has for us, and it sets us free to live in his fullness. That's why Paul wrote in Galatians 5 that all God's laws are satisfied as we learn to love others.

Throughout this book I've emphasized that we remain in Jesus by being where he is. We've talked already about his presence in our worship and communion in prayer with him, and the wisdom of Scripture that reveals who he is. Now Jesus' instruction to us to love one another brings us to two more places where we engage his presence: in the community of believers and with people in need.

For where two or three come together in my name, there am I with them. (Matthew 18:20) Jesus is present where believers come together to share his life. I'm talking way beyond church membership or attendance. Sitting in a large gathering watching all the action happen onstage doesn't even begin to approach the power of Jesus' invitation here.

Body life in the New Testament was not observed in carefully planned meetings—it was celebrated in close friendships. The early believers lived out their faith through intimate and mutually supportive contact with other believers. You will find it easier to grow in intimacy with Jesus if you have a circle of believers whose lives you can touch two or three times a week and with whom you can be authentic as you share encouragement, insight, and opportunities to love one another.

Nothing will bring us to freedom faster than loving the people around us through the most menial forms of service and looking for ways to encourage others. The world teaches us to be preoccupied with our own needs and ambitions. Jesus, however, offered us the opportunity to lay down our lives for him by being a blessing to others. Learning to love that way reverses the corruption that is in the world. No longer preoccupied with our own desires, we become part of God's work to touch others.

This is an interesting vineyard Jesus described. It is a one-vine vineyard. Every branch grows from the same vine—Jesus. And no branch lives independent from the others. When one is besieged, they all are. When one is in need, the others can help make up the difference. I've seen entire branches stripped of their leaves by voracious insects. Not a leaf left on the branch—and without leaves grapes won't sweeten. But these still did. Why? Because the sugar produced by the other branches on that vine found its way to the grapes on the denuded branch.

We were never meant to thrive in this kingdom on our own. Trying to do so is the same as being a one-person softball team. No matter how good you are, there's no way you can win a ball game by yourself. How can you cover the whole field on defense? You'd have to strike out every batter and hit a home run when you came to bat. Who's capable of that?

Supportive, intimate friendships, opportunities to serve, added wisdom and strength, lessons of forgiveness, and a place to be held accountable all grow out of our relationships with other believers and are all helpful in our growth in him. Let's not forget his command. It wasn't to get love from others, but *to love others.*

The last place Jesus clearly said he invested his presence was in ministry to people at points of their need. *Whatever you did for one of the least of these brothers of mine, you did for me.* (Matthew 25:40) He affirms his presence in the needs of his creation and tells us that our response to people in need, not just believers, is a response to him. We have been blessed by God to be a blessing to others.

Everyone who grows in friendship with Jesus will find regular opportunities to serve others in the daily course of their lives and will seek out opportunities to go into another person's world and serve. You don't have to go out of the country for these opportunities. Serving in a soup kitchen or tutoring an underprivileged child at your neighborhood school can be every bit as powerful as going on an outreach in Asia.

True Christ-like love is foreign to our flesh and in the beginning it will be difficult to learn how to lay our lives down. But learning to live in love's freedom is one of the great pleasures of being a branch in this vineyard. It is deeply fulfilling and full of surprises. We'll find ourselves doing and saying things to others that will astound us. "That's not me" and "I've never felt like this before" will become common refrains of wonder . . . all because we have learned to listen to his nudge to "die to it" in the midst of great joy or frustration.

Chapter 39

Trained Up for Fruitfulness

No discipline seems pleasant at the time, but painful.
Later on, however, it produces a harvest of righteousness
and peace for those who have been trained by it.
HEBREWS 12:11

Not a season goes by when there isn't *something* the farmer has to do in order to have a fruitful vineyard. Many plants will bear some fruit in the wild, but not the grapevine. It cannot even support its own branches. They must be painstakingly tied on a wire to keep the fruit and canes off of the ground. If it is not pruned every year, all the energy of the vine will be spent producing leaves, and not fruit. So month after month the farmer is in the vineyard.

In my father's vineyard a long, shiny wire runs the length of each vineyard row. Held in place by stakes driven into the ground next to each vine, it is a simple but lifesaving tool. It supports the canes above the vine so they won't break under the foliage and fruit of the new season.

All of that fruit weighs a significant amount, and since the canes arc gracefully up from the vine, the load will pull them to the point where the cane will either split or break from the branch altogether. Either way the fruit would be lost, a victim of the cane's success.

So, the last thing the farmer does in winter is to wrap the canes around the wire. Two canes from each vine run down the wire in one direction and three go in the opposite direction. When a row is tied on the wire it looks as if an unending cane stretches the length of the field. Everything is in a straight line, and any canes left untied look so out of place that they are noticeable from a great distance.

This tying is not a difficult task for the farmer, but it is for the canes. They are almost a year old now and not at all as pliable as they used to be. Their woody grain makes them quite rigid, and the farmer's attempts to curve them back to the wire and wrap them around it is often met with resistance. The canes try to slip from the farmer's grasp and protest with popping and snapping as he reins them in.

Here's where the worker must be careful. If he pulls on a cane too abruptly or at the wrong angle the cane will break off, and one-fifth of the crop of that vine will be lost—remember, the excess canes were pruned away earlier. The farmer must take the cane in hand and curve it gently back to the wire in an arc that will not break it. Gentleness is of the utmost importance.

The cane would prefer to remain free, able to reach out to the heavens unrestricted by the wire and the other canes it is tied with. It doesn't know how much it needs the wire because it doesn't need it right now. Only when the fruit begins to ripen will it need that support. By then, however, it will be too late to wrap the cane on the wire without breaking the cane or tearing off the grapes.

Training isn't easy for us either. The writer of Hebrews reminds us how unpleasant it is, and how we can easily resist his hand of discipline mistaking it for a foreign presence that means us harm. If we haven't learned to follow him even when he asks something difficult of us, the process of fruitfulness will be stunted before a new season even begins. Though it is not pleasant at the time, the benefits of discipline bring great joy and freedom to our lives.

Those who don't surrender to his discipline will find their life in him incredibly frustrating. It will be filled with promise, but those promises will never come to fullness because they cannot sustain the fruitfulness God wants to give. We've all known people who seemed incredibly godly until they became successful in some way, and then we watched that success become their undoing. Either pride or selfishness ran rampant beneath the surface.

All too many times people have told me such a story and ended it with, "I just don't understand. How can God use someone like that so powerfully and have it end this way?" Because they had not submitted to the Father's hand, their success overwhelmed their character and they ended up focused on themselves and their own success, and they became destructive to those around them. Remember, the real fruit of the vineyard is the transformation of our character so that Jesus' life takes shape in us.

Unless we learn from his discipline, we won't have the support around us to sustain his work. All too often people sense God's calling in their hearts, and then set out to accomplish it in their own strength or by their own plans. Though they may find some measure of external success in their own efforts, the true fruitfulness they anticipated never comes.

The apostle Paul wrestled with this issue in his letter to the Corinthians.

> *Everyone who competes in the games goes into strict training. They do it to get a crown that will not last; but we do it to get a crown that will last forever.*
> — 1 CORINTHIANS 9:25

He used the analogy of a boxer who will, without discipline, go through all the right motions but still not achieve the prize. Therefore, Paul said, he trained diligently in spiritual matters to insure that his vision followed through to fruitfulness. And so must we.

But what is that discipline? Most incorrectly assume it is a series of spiritual disciplines or religious rituals or activities. We know how to busy ourselves with those things . . . but they always disappoint us when our lives are as empty at the end of those things as when we began.

Discipline for the vine is learning how to live in a growing relationship with the Father through the work of the Son. It isn't as simple as observing a set of disciplines or rituals. That relationship is primarily stirred in the heart by a passionate desire to know him and a willingness to surrender our lives to his will.

Learn to commune with him! Just because you know *what* God wants to do, don't assume you know *how* he wants to do it. Whatever God is calling you to focus on, make sure that this goal stays at the top of your prayer list. Salt it with prayer all the time. In doing so, listen to God. When he wants to accomplish something in your life he will give you simple steps to follow to bring that plan about.

Learn to follow him. Write down things God seems to be nudging you toward and follow through with them. At some points that may mean we make choices that don't seem to us in the moment to be in our best interest. Remember, those who seek to save their life on this journey end up losing it, while those who are willing to lose it will find what true life really means.

It is in the midst of adversity and extremity that we truly learn how to rely on him instead of relying on ourselves. I don't know how many times I've sensed God nudging me a certain direction, but blocked it out because it seemed too difficult or painful a road to go down. Instead I plodded along by my own wisdom, ignoring what he told me to do. Only in the resulting mess do I recognize my folly and turn back to him. Just because something is difficult doesn't mean that he isn't in it, or that what we're learning in the midst of pain is vital to his continuing work of transformation in us.

Invite some other believers to come alongside you in prayer and honest dialogue as God fulfills his work. They can help confirm the validity of what you're hearing thereby insuring that it is not the result of a wild imagination. They can also hold you accountable to the steps of obedience that God gives you. Without supportive relationships of loving believers few of us will follow through enough to really find fruitfulness.

The emphasis here is on supportive relationships. Too many of us have had experiences with believers judging us, criticizing us with jealousy, or wanting to use us. Supportive relationships are built on encouragement. Out of a sincere concern for your welfare and growth in Christ, they embrace genuineness and honesty.

With your canes firmly wrapped around these supports you can rest confidently, knowing that God will be able to complete his work in you. Take hope; winter is almost over. Rested and restaged, the vine is ready for another season of growth.

We have now come to the waning days of winter. It is only mid-February, but in the short winters of California's San Joaquin Valley, spring is just around the corner. It has already been in the 70s earlier this afternoon, urging the winter to succumb to the ever-lengthening days.

This is where we began many pages ago. We've come around to it again, for spring with its burst of joy and fresh vision is just around the corner. As the days lengthen, a new year in the vineyard is about to begin!

Chapter 40

Be Fruitful

He has made everything beautiful in its time.
He has also set eternity in the hearts of men;
yet they cannot fathom what God has done from beginning to end.
ECCLESIASTES 3:11

The seasons of the vineyard demonstrate different ways that God works with us, but of course he is far more creative than the illustration allows. We have looked at some of the ways God works in our lives, not only so we won't be surprised when they happen, but also so we'll know how to respond to him when they do.

Don't be surprised if they don't fit so neatly into a box. Rarely do I find my life exclusively in one season or another. God's work in me at any one time may be a blending of different facets of these seasons. In my own life I find God calling me to endurance in some areas where fruit is maturing . . . but in other areas (where my own efforts have taken over for God) I see him with pruning shears in hand. In other areas, fresh growth is breaking out.

I still encounter circumstances I don't fully understand. I sometimes endure periods where I'm not sure at all what God is doing, but by hanging in there, I'll eventually see how he works all things out for good. This is all part of the dynamic of following after God's heart in this age. God does different things at different times:

Even though we may not understand it now, God moves with a plan, and what burns in our hearts is far larger than our mind will comprehend. It is sufficient for us to know that he will make all things, including our hopes and visions, beautiful in his time.

In the meantime, pursue your friendship with Jesus at all costs. Continue to carve out meaningful time with him regardless of the distractions of this age. Settle for nothing less than fullness of joy welling up within when you can see his glory produced through you and made available to a dying generation.

Jesus' simple summary of John 15 will suffice for this work as well: "Go and bear fruit." When it's all said and done, what matters is the fruit we have borne for the kingdom of God, purchased by our friendship with him and expressed in our transformed lives.

My prayer is that this message—"Go and bear fruit"—will fill your heart with a desire never to settle for anything less than a growing fullness of joy in your relationship with him, and the fruit that results from such fulfillment. I hope it stimulates hunger in your heart and broadens your perspective of what it means to be a branch on the vine in the Father's vineyard.

I AM *the true vine,*
and my Father is the gardener.
He cuts off every branch in me that bears no fruit,
while every branch that does bear fruit he prunes
so that it will be even more fruitful.

You are already clean
because of the word I have spoken to you.
Remain in me, and I will remain in you.
No branch can bear fruit by itself; it must remain
in the vine.
Neither can you bear fruit
unless you remain in me.

I am the vine;
you are the branches.
If a man remains in me and I in him,
he will bear much fruit;
apart from me you can do nothing.
If anyone does not remain in me,
he is like a branch that is thrown away and withers;
Such branches are picked up,
thrown into the fire and burned.

If you remain in me and my words remain in you,
ask whatever you wish, and it will be given you.
This is to my Father's glory, that you bear much fruit,
showing yourselves to be my disciples.

As the Father has loved me,
so have I loved you.
Now remain in my love.
If you obey my commands,
you will remain in my love,
Just as I have obeyed my Father's commands
and remain in his love.

I have told you this so that my joy may be in you
and that your joy may be complete.
My command is this: Love each other
as I have loved you.
Greater love has no one than this,
that he lay down his life for his friends.
You are my friends if you do what I command.

I no longer call you servants,
because a servant does not know his master's business.
Instead, I have called you friends,
for everything that I learned from my Father
I have made known to you.
You did not choose me, but I chose you
and appointed you to go and bear fruit—
fruit that will last.
Then the Father will give you
whatever you ask in my name.
This is my command: Love each other.

Acknowledgments

I am grateful for the wonderful people God has put in my life to encourage, enlighten, and share my journey. That includes dear friends all over the world and the men and women who make up the board of Lifestream Ministries who oversee all that I do.

This is the fourth expression of this material that has been so significant in my life. Every time I walk in a vineyard or see one referred to in Scripture, I am drawn back to the earliest days of my life and the wonder and simplicity of the gifts of God in my life every day.

No one shares that with me more than my wife of thirty-six years, Sara. She has been my companion, collaborator, friend, and partner through all the twists and turns that circumstances have thrown our way. I will always be grateful for the joy we share together and the price she has paid to share this journey with me.

And finally, Jessica Glasner, who edited this book for me and helped shape it from my earlier writings on the vineyard. In her capable hands, this book has found life again and I am deeply indebted to her and grateful for her skills.